The Real Estate Book

The Real Estate Book

Donna Kay Cindy Kakonge

Donna Kay Kakonge, MA, ABD
2017

Dedication

Dedicated to all my family who worked so hard to own homes in North America.

Acknowledgements

I would like to thank my teachers, my editor, my creative writing course classmates, and my family without whose help this book would never have been completed.

Thank you for your patience and guidance, your use of the editor's red pen, especially to Mrs. Chen. Thank you for the "outstanding," I am always striving to reach that again.

CHAPTER ONE: BECOMING A REAL ESTATE PROFESSIONAL

IN THIS CHAPTER YOU WILL

- Establish what it takes to become a successful real estate professional
- Understand the requirements for Licensure
- Understand the process involved in becoming a real estate professional
- The importance of having a good character to be a real estate professional
- The continuing education involved for becoming a real estate professional

VOCABULARY TO KNOW

- Advisory Council
- Affidavit of Non-Participation
- Attorney in Fact
- Broker
- Continuing Education
- Exchange Company
- Good Moral Character
- Hotel Operator
- Inoperative
- Leasing Agent
- Licensure
- Managing Broker
- Medium of Advertising
- Multiple Listing Service
- Nonrefundable
- Resident Lessee
- Resident Manager
- Sole Proprietor
- Sponsoring Broker
- Timeshare Owner

Requirements for Licensure

According to the individual's states Real Estate License Acts, companies which are limited liability partnerships, corporations, limited liability companies, partnerships or individuals, with the exception of a leasing agent, which will be discussed in more detail later in this chapter, must be licensed if they are entering into real estate transactions **for another** or **for compensation** under the following conditions:

- Lease real estate, rent, purchase, sell or exchange or offers regarding these transactions
- Negotiation of real estate
- Renovations to real estate or buy or sell options or agreements regarding these transactions
- Managing the collection of rent
- Advertising related to real estate transactions
- Procuring leads and prospects and assisting in these matters
- Real estate that is open to the public for the purposes of marketing
- Real estate transactions at an auction

If brokers are not licensed, they must sign an **affidavit of non-participation**.

Exemptions

There are some exceptions regarding licensure under the Real Estate License Acts for various states within the United States.

Acting on Behalf of the Owner or as an Owner

When acting on behalf of an owner or as the owner, a leasing agent is exempt from licensure. Here are the exemptions that are connected with ownership and owners:

- When an owner takes on the role as a broker
- When someone is a **resident manager** of the owner, potentially an employee of the owner
- A **resident lessee**, someone who is leasing the owner's property and acting on behalf of the owner – in some buildings this person is known to be the superintendent

- A **timeshare owner** that acts on behalf of the owner

Acting as a Professional Real Estate Broker

Exemptions that concern real estate professionals are as follows:
- Acting under a power of attorney, an **attorney in fact**
- Court order actions
- Under the Real Estate Timeshare Act of 1999, an **exchange company**
- Anyone operating under the Auction License Act
- **Hotel operators**

Involvement in Information Collection and Dissemination Purposes

The following are examples of when there would be involvement in information collection and dissemination purposes:
- **Multiple Listing Service** which advertises properties which are for sale
- Advertising the property, also known as a **medium of advertising**

Real Estates Licenses

Throughout the many states in the United States there are many different types of **real estate licenses**. Here are some in the following:

Broker

A **Broker** is someone who assists the managing broker and is compensated through the sponsoring broker in order to do their work regarding real estate transactions. Much of the knowledge required in doing this work effectively will be discussed later in this chapter as well as in subsequent chapters. Below is information regarding the requirements involved for receiving a broker's license:
- The age requirement is 21, however if someone who is 18 has completed high school, they are eligible to apply for a broker's license

- A certificate from a high school that lasted in length for four years, or its recognizable equivalent
- A potential broker and brokers themselves must be of good moral character
- A completed sponsor form
- Completed and signed application form
- Passing the examination issued by the Division
- Paying the non-refundable fee for the application and the exam

Good Moral Character

In order to obtain a broker's license, a potential licensee cannot have any of the following and then they will be considered of good moral character:
- Revocation of a license previously
- Adhere to all of the codes of conduct under the Real Estate Act
- Been convicted of a crime of fraud
- Been convicted of any felony

Salesperson to Broker License Transition

The salesperson would need to complete 30 hours of approved education, as well as pass an exam by the Division.

Maintenance of Broker's License

Once a license is obtained, here is the key information required to maintain the license:
- Once meeting the requirements for a license and all fees are paid, the broker will be issued a pocket card
- Paying the fees for the license
- Continuing education (much of what will be covered as an introduction throughout this book)
- No more than six hours of continuing education within a calendar year

- Renewing the license in person within seven days and through the mail in 10 days
- A license that has been expired for two years or more is no longer valid
- Not been convicted of any felony

Managing Broker

The **managing broker** is the boss of the broker and is appointed by the sponsoring brokerage firm. The following are the requirements for the managing broker license.

Application Requirements for a Managing Broker

The minimum requirements are as follows:
- A minimum of 21 years of age
- Be of good moral character
- Evidence of graduation from a four year high school or its accepted equivalency
- Passing the examination administered by the Division
- Paying the non-refundable fee
- Completed and signed application form
- Issued by the sponsoring broker or brokerage firm, a form allowing the managing broker to examine and audit special accounts
- Current admittance to the practice of law
- Graduation from the pre-licensing education

Requirements for Pre-Licensing Education

A managing broker must complete 165 hours of education in order to be eligible to have a license as a managing broker.

Examination

From the time a managing broker passes the examination administered by the Division, they have one year to complete the requirements regarding licensure. An applicant can take the test four times.

Transitional for Post-Licensing

For brokers, the transitional educational requirements are 45 hours to become a managing broker.

Requirements for Continuing Education

For each two-year renewal period of a managing broker's license, they are required to have 24 hours of continuing education in order to renew their license.

Reciprocity

The term reciprocity in this sense has a meaning that a broker or a managing broker who is licensed in one jurisdiction can also be licensed in a different jurisdiction. There are certain states that have this reciprocal agreement

Leasing Agent

A leasing agent deals solely with leasing residential real estate is employed by a real estate brokerage firm.

Application Requirements for Leasing Agents

The following are the minimum requirements involved to obtain a license to become a leasing agent:

- A minimum of 18 years of age
- Proof of graduation from a four year high school or its recognized equivalency
- Be of good moral character
- Properly completed and submitted sponsor form
- Completed and signed application form
- Passing the examination set forth by the Division

- Non-refundable fee paid in full

Requirements for Pre-Licensing

A leasing agent needs to complete 15 hours of study by a recognized an approved organization.

Continuing Education Requirements

The requirements are set forth by the Advisory Council and Board.

Sponsorship of Licensee

Sponsoring brokers, or real estate brokerage firms, issue licenses to brokers, managing brokers and to leasing agents. Some points to note is that a broker, managing broker or leasing agent can only be under the employ of one sponsoring broker at a time. A licensee can receive compensation only from their sponsoring broker. A sponsoring broker can be a person and/or a legal organization such as a partnership, corporation or various types of companies.

Sponsorship Transfer

If a licensee accepts sponsorship from a different and a new sponsoring broker, the following needs to be done within 24 hours to ensure effective and obligated duties regarding sponsorship transfer:
- Sponsor card in duplicate
- Endorsed license of licensee or affidavit stating why it is not given up
- Administrative fees

The license is instantly given **inoperative** status.

Sponsorship Termination

When an employment contract between a licensee and a sponsoring broker is terminated by either party, the following steps must be taken:

- The sponsoring broker must activate the original license of the licensee and state the reasons for termination
- The sponsoring broker must surrender within two days (2 days), a copy of the license and also give a copy of that license to Department of Financial and Professional Regulation as it applies to the particular state in question

Status Types of Licenses

A broker's license can be in the following classifications:

- Active
- Denied
- Expired or Inactive
- Inoperative
- Probationary
- Revoked
- Suspended

Summary

The licensure process protects the public and the same time is meant to hold high standards for licensees for effective, competent and ethical and legal work to be done regarding real estate transactions. There are requirements for brokers, managing brokers and licensing agents. The minimum requirements that are consistent with all of these licensures are that the applicant have graduated from high school, pass an examination set forth by the Division, as well as complete the necessary forms and pay the necessary fees. Brokers may work for a sponsoring broker and there are a set of guidelines set forth if this relationship is either transferred and/or terminated.

Quiz

1. What is the Advisory Council?
2. What is an affidavit of non-participation?
3. Describe in detail how a broker obtains their license?
4. Describe the transition from broker to managing broker?
5. Describe in detail how a managing broker obtains their license?
6. What is a sponsoring broker?
7. Describe in detail how a licensing agent gets their license?
8. How much continuing education is involved with the licensures mentioned in this chapter?
9. What is an exchange company?
10. Why is good moral character important for a broker and its related fields?
11. What is the Multiple Listing Service?
12. What is a resident lessee?
13. What is a timeshare owner?
14. How long does it take to become a managing broker?
15. Do you need to be a lawyer to be a managing broker? *True or False*

CHAPTER TWO: VARIOUS KINDS OF AGENCY RELATIONSHIPS

Agency Relationships

Whatever the principal could do themselves a **universal agent** can do.

Regarding a broad range of issues related to the business activity of a sponsoring broker, this is what a **general agent** does.

With detailed instructions and regarding a specific business activity, **special agents** work on these projects.

A **designated agent** is appointed to help or to act on behalf of a certain principal.

Single Agency

When an agent is representing one sole party in a real estate transaction, this is called **single agency**.

Buyer Agency

When an agency represents buyers of real estate primarily, this is known as a **buyer agency**.

Property Management Agency

The owner of any given real estate may employ a brokerage firm and/or sponsoring broker to manage, lease, and handle all of the business activities of their real estate, otherwise known as a **property management agency**.

Dual Agency

Within a **dual agency** as it concerns a sponsoring broker, the same agency represents both parties in the purchase and the sale of real estate.

Disclosed Dual Agency

Dual agency is permitted only if the buyer and the seller are aware that there is dual agency occurring.

Dual Agency and Consent

In some of the states within the United States, the practice of dual agency is illegal and requires written consent on the both the parties of the buyer and the seller.

Undisclosed Dual Agency

Dual agency cannot be intentional.

Disclosure of Agency

Disclosure is imperative to the work that real estate agents do in regards to which they are representing. Guaranteed sales plans, financial irresponsibility, returned checks and fees, failure to disclose interest, unlicensed practice, and unauthorized practice of law comprise other violations that can result in discipline under the Illinois Real Estate License Act and the Rules of the Department of Financial and Professional Regulation.

Customer-Level Services

The main obligations that a real estate agent has is to their principal, however they also must be obliged to third parties and practice the same standards outlined by their licensing bodies and upholding ethical standards.

Summary

Whatever the principal could do themselves a universal agent can do. Regarding a broad range of issues related to the business activity of a sponsoring broker, this is what a general agent does. With detailed instructions and regarding a specific business activity, special agents work on these projects. A designated agent is appointed to help or to act on behalf of a certain principal.

Disclosure is imperative to the work that real estate agents do in regards to which they are representing. Guaranteed sales plans, financial irresponsibility, returned checks and fees, failure to disclose interest, unlicensed practice, and unauthorized practice of law comprise other violations that can result in discipline under the Illinois Real Estate License Act and the Rules of the Department of Financial and Professional Regulation.

The main obligations that a real estate agent has is to their principal, however they also must be obliged to third parties and practice the same standards outlined by their licensing bodies and upholding ethical standards.

Quiz

1. What is buyer agency?
2. What are the different types of buyer agency?
3. What is meant by confirmation of consent to dual agency?
4. What are customer-level services?
5. What is a designated agent?
6. What is disclosed dual agency?
7. What is disclosure of agency?
8. What is dual agency?
9. What is a general agent?
10. What does a property management agency do?
11. What does a single agency do?
12. What is a special agent?
13. What is undisclosed dual agency?
14. What is a universal agent?

CHAPTER THREE: UNDERSTANDING LEGAL DEFINITIONS

IN THIS CHAPTER YOU WILL

- Recognize and define the three key terms for real estate law
- Know how surveys are conducted
- Be able to present on how a rectangular survey description works for your class
- Identify the various components of land measurement
- Have a deeper understanding of real estate law for your own practice or for personal knowledge
- Demonstrate through exercises at the end of the chapter what you have learned

VOCABULARY TO KNOW

- Air Lot
- Base Line
- Benchmark
- Correction Line
- Datum
- Fractional Section
- Government Check
- Government Lot
- Legal Description
- Lot-and-block System
- Meters-and-bounds Method
- Monument
- Plat Map
- Point of Beginning (POB)
- Principle Meridian
- Range
- Rectangular Survey System
- Section
- Survey

- Township
- Township Line
- Township Tier

Describing Land

Although landowners and people who own real estate believe that they should own all of the land that they are paying for or is paid for there are other important aspects that come into play that are not just as simple as owning the land. People who have real estate licenses need to understand the key and specific legal terms involved with that land that they own.

Historically, the names of streets in any location all over America can sometimes be renamed after a notable figure that has changed history. Just having the name of a street is not legally binding to prove ownership of a property and ownership of land. As well, deeds, mortgages and changes in ownership of land and property shift and evolve over time, making understanding the concrete and binding laws behind describing land extremely important.

What is a **legal description**? Legal descriptions help a court of law with deeds and mortgages so they are understood clearly by the legal system. The information that is gathered to describe land is done through a **survey** – there are measurements and descriptors used, as well as techniques of this survey to assess land. Surveys also help to set the boundaries that are present around a certain piece of land so it is not confused by the ownership of land that may be owned by someone else close by. Surveys also help to determine the precise location of land that is owned as well. If a surveyor can find the piece of land – this adequate for the courts and legally binding. Many other methods other than an address of a street are used to locate and to identify land. A surveyor cannot determine property based on just an address; there are many other elements that are used to determine land, to describe land and to define land.

Descriptions and Methodology Used for Real Estate

There are three methods used for defining real estate:
- Lot and Block (recorded plat)
- Metes-and-Bounds

- Rectangular or Government Survey

These methods are often used separately; however there are several instances when these methods are combined. In the United States there are some states that use all three of these methods to describe real estate, in other states they use just one of the methods above.

In the original 13 colonies of the United States the metes-and-bounds method was used. During this time period of the 13 colonies, the rectangular or government survey method was coming into formation. Recently, technology has helped to add more precision to land measurements, using satellites and computer-assisted design techniques. Going back in time first, we will begin by discussing the **metes-and-bounds method**.

The Method of Metes-and-Bounds

This method is the oldest method. The definition of the word is that *metes* is defined as distance and still sometimes used in sports vocabulary. The definition of bounds is angles or compass direction. This method heavily relies on a property's or the land's physical dimensions in order for it to work effectively. With this method, it always starts at the beginning of the land, or **point of beginning (POB)**. From that POB, the surveyor then moves around the property and/or land to measure the rest of the land or property. Boundaries are defined in a linear framework and landmarks (*monuments*) are used as well as directions to determine and to define the land. The end of the surveyor's job in measuring with metes-and-bounds method is at the POB. This way the entire piece of land has been surveyed and recorded for its measurements. Next, we will discuss the monuments, also known as landmarks of a piece of land.

Description of Monuments

An important part of land surveying and describing land involves monuments. Monuments are stationary elements on a property or piece of land that will help to mark the POB, the finishing parts of boundaries and partitions, as well as the position of boundaries which intersect. A monument can come from nature, such as a lake, a hill or a tree. A monument can also be man-made such as a highway, a sign post or a street. For legal reasons, monuments come with additional notes by surveyors of being "more or less" for their locations. The reasons for this is because the fact they exist is more important than their size and/or measurements, however the distance is of the upmost importance.

Below there is an example of the metes-and-bounds method for a piece of land in Springfield, Tennessee.

Figure 2.1 follows:

The piece of land below is described as running 400 feet west and east along Highway 524. The tract of land is also 250 feet north and south along Interstate 81. The monuments are man-made and are highways.

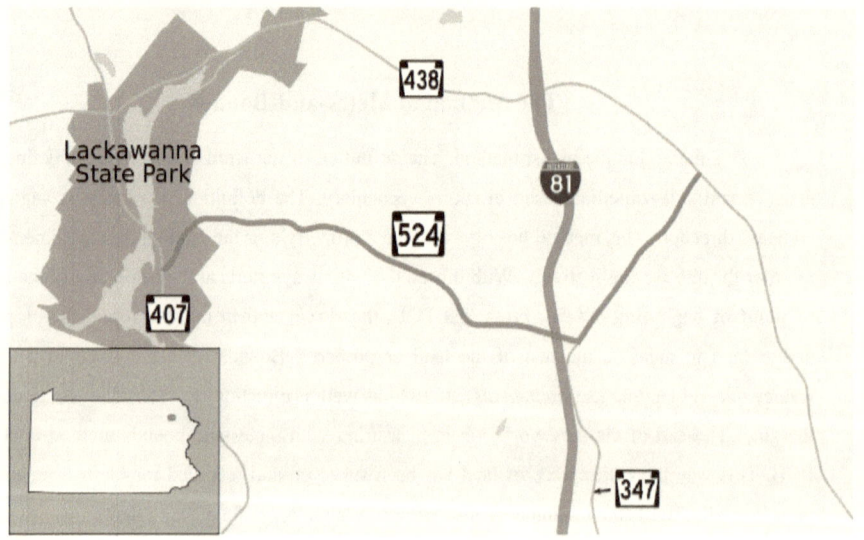

Here is an example of when the metes-and-bounds method is used to describe a piece of land in a court of law:

> Starting at the point of the intersect of Highways 524 and Interstate 81, the land continues east along Highway 524 close to Lackawanna State Park and south down Interstate 81. The land then circles back up northwest to Highway 524 and then north on Interstate 81 coming back to the point of beginning where Interstate 81 and Highways 524 intersect.

As surveyors use this method in a court of law, this metes-and-bounds method can lead to a lot of ambiguity. It truly should be used with caution. Sometimes the information can be very complex including compass directions and as natural elements of the environment erode such as trees, lakes and hills, this method can become obsolete for determining the true definition of land. This method requires surveyors who are trained and experienced with their jobs, particularly when it comes to legal matters.

In Texas

A state that was an independent republic before the United States was formed on July 4, 1776 is Texas. Due to this the land method primarily used in Texas is metes-and-bounds.

The following section will describe the rectangular survey system.

Method of the Rectangular Survey System

This method was formed in 1785 by Congress and is also known as The Public Land Survey System (PLSS), however more commonly referred to as the **rectangular survey system**. Two lines are the basis of this method for defining land: base lines and principle meridians. The **base lines** go east and west and the **principle meridians** go north and south. Using the example from 2.1 above, Highway 524 close to Lackawanna State Park would be the base line and Interstate 81 would be the principle meridian. Both of these points of reference, principle meridians and base lines are calculated based on longitude and latitude. The principle meridians have a name and they have a number and they intersect with a baseline. Each baseline that joins with a principle meridian is used to define land for court purposes. All of this latter information is also included on a boundary lines map. Currently, there exist 37 principle meridians throughout the United States, not including Hawaii or Puerto Rico.

Principle meridians help to determine the boundaries of a piece of land. Pieces of land are only determined by one principle meridian and not necessarily the nearest principle meridian.

In the United States

The boundaries for the states between the United States are based on the principles of meridians that run north and south. Using the rectangular system method, the legal definition of what constitutes the United States is indicated in the north and south lines below in Figure 2.2:

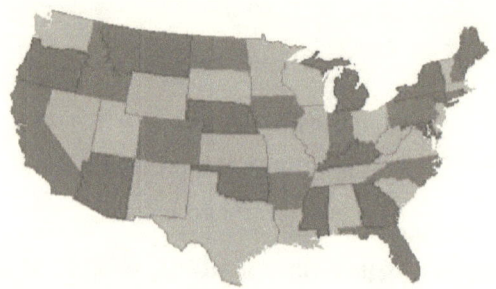

Other dividers that are used to indicate the definition of land in the rectangular system method, similar to metes-and-bounds method are:

- Quarter-section Lines
- Ranges
- Sections
- Townships

Township Tiers

When there are demarcation lines that run east and west and are also parallel to the base line that also run six miles apart – these are known as **township tiers**. They also form pieces of land. The piece of land that is seven base lines north from Gott St. to the top of Luke Blvd is approximately the distance of a six mile township tier in Figure 2.3 below.

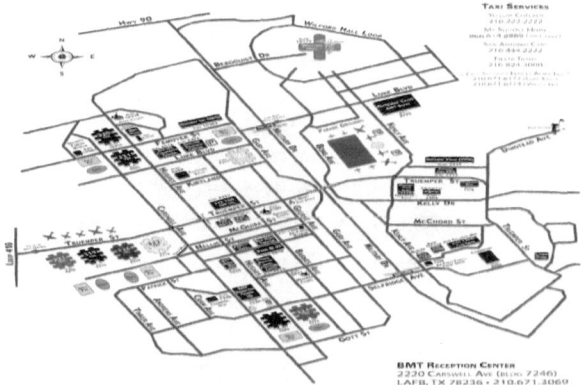

In the following we will discuss **ranges**.

Ranges

The definition of land that measures six miles and is also parallel to the principle meridian is known as a range. Using the example of Figure 2.3 above, from Gott St. to Luke Blvd. would be a range, and moving further north of Luke Blvd. would be the start of another range. Next, we will discuss township squares.

Township Squares

As the horizontal lines in the rectangular survey system connect with the vertical lines of the range, this is what is known as township squares. Township squares consist of six miles, as mentioned previously and are 36 square miles, or in other forms of distance measurements 23,040 acres.

There are legal definitions for every township that include the following:
- Definition of the range of land
- The definition of the township tier, as well as where the township is placed on the map
- The number and/or name of the principle meridian for where the township is located on a map

Next, we will discuss sections as they relate to the rectangular survey system.

Sections

Within each township there are 36 sections. The distance of each **section** is one square mile or 640 acres. In Figure 2.4 below, the beginning of the sections always start from the northeast corner indicated by the number 1. Section 16 is highlighted because this section tends to be used for building schools and is set aside for schools.

North

6	5	4	3	2	1
7	8	9	10	11	12
18	17	**16**	15	14	13
19	20	21	22	23	24
30	29	28	27	26	25
31	32	33	34	35	36

Correction Lines

Since the earth is not flat, it is round; range lines are not always exactly parallel to one another and will often curve upwards to reach the North Pole. Correction lines are used to accommodate for this situation. **Correction lines** are applied to every fourth line of a township north and sound of the baseline. There are guide meridians that are 24 miles apart from the principle meridian and a 24 mile square irregular area that are the result of these fixes to compensate for the earth's surface are known as a **government check**.

Any changes made to a section based on the north and the west boundaries are known as **fractional sections**. The other sections are called **standard sections**.

Government Lots and Fractional Sections

Fractional sections are sections that are too big or too small. Sometimes this can occur because different surveyors have worked on the rectangular survey system to measure the land's definition, or in other cases part of the land could be covered in a body of water. Small pieces of land are given a number and are known as **government lots**. Here is an example of how a government lot would be written down by a surveyor:

> *Government Lot 5, the southwest corner of fractional Section 14, Township 3 East, Range 8 West, of the Lackawanna State Park Meridian.*

How to Read a Rectangular Survey Description

In order to understand what a surveyor writes down concerning the land definition of a property with the rectangular survey method, you would need to read the instructions of the surveyor backwards, moving from the right to the left rather than the left to the right as you would normally read. Here is an example of a surveyor's notes regarding a property based on the rectangular survey system below:

> *The E½ of the SE½ of the NE½ of Section 27, Township 3 South, Range 18 East of the Sixth Principal Meridian.*

As mentioned previously, moving from the right to the left rather than the left to the right, in order to find this piece of land you would begin with the Sixth Principal Meridian and then continue onwards moving left along the descriptor. For the rectangular survey method, the more lengthy the description of the land is would indicate that the land measurements are smaller. For legal purposes, descriptions for this method also include the state and the country where the land is found because there can be more than one base line connected to the meridians.

The Indication of the Metes-and-Bounds Method in the Rectangular Survey Method

An example of a state in the United States that uses both the metes-and-bounds method and the rectangular survey method is Ohio. There are three situations that would arise that would require the need for the combination of these two methods: a piece of land that is too small to be partitioned into quarter sections, when a piece of land is irregular, or when a piece of land does not follow the surveyor's descriptors. Here is an example of what a surveyor would write when combining these two methods below:

> Part of the southwest corner of Section 16 (remembering that Section 16 is always designated for schools), Township 34 South, Range 10 East of the Ninth Principal Meridian, with a boundary of a line described in the following: beginning at the northwest corner of the southwest corner of Section 16 then south 800 feet; then east parallel with the north line of the aforementioned section 200 feet; then north parallel with the south line of the aforementioned section 300 feet to the north line of the aforementioned southwest corner; then east along the north line to the point of beginning.

Irregular and small tracts are described by both a combination of the rectangular survey method and the metes-and-bounds method. Here is a visual example in Figure 2.5 below:

Lot-and-Block Method

This section will discuss the third land definition method, the **lot-and-block method** which is also referred to as the *recorded plat system*. This method relies on maps of public record in the United States that indicate the lots and the blocks of a piece of land. The maps that are of public record are known as *plat maps*. This method is useful for land that resides in suburban areas and in urban areas.

There are two steps that a land surveyor uses in the lot-and-block method. The first thing that is done is that a piece of land is defined either through the rectangular survey method, the metes-and-bounds method or a combination of both. The large pieces of land which results from these land definitions are partitioned into smaller parts of land. Due to this, the lot-and-block method tends to have land measurements which are decreased from those of the metes-and-bounds method and the rectangular survey method.

For the lot-and-block method, the lot refers to the number associated with the piece of land and the block is the name of the subdivision in the location where the land resides. The references of a "block" come from the early 1900s based on urban settings in the United States.

Licensed surveyors and/or engineers start their surveys of land with a *subdivision plat*. As mentioned previously, a subdivision plat is a map that helps the licensed surveyors and/or engineers to guide them in their assessment of the land measurements to conclude with a legal definition of the land. These plats are derived from the aforementioned other land definition methods used: metes-and-bounds method and rectangular survey method. The subdivision plats are much smaller in size than the measurements taken for the metes-and-bounds method and the rectangular survey method. Licensed surveyors and/or engineers then record all of lots and blocks according to the applicable numbers, letters, streets, roads, highways, interstates, and describe the land according to the laws of the county or township where the piece of land is located. This information then becomes public record once it is approved by legal officials such as judges and local government administrative staff to ensure that it has met all of the requirements for the land definition. A simple example to illustrate a subdivision plat is from the Market Street illustration below in Figure 2.6 of a subdivision plat:

Market Street

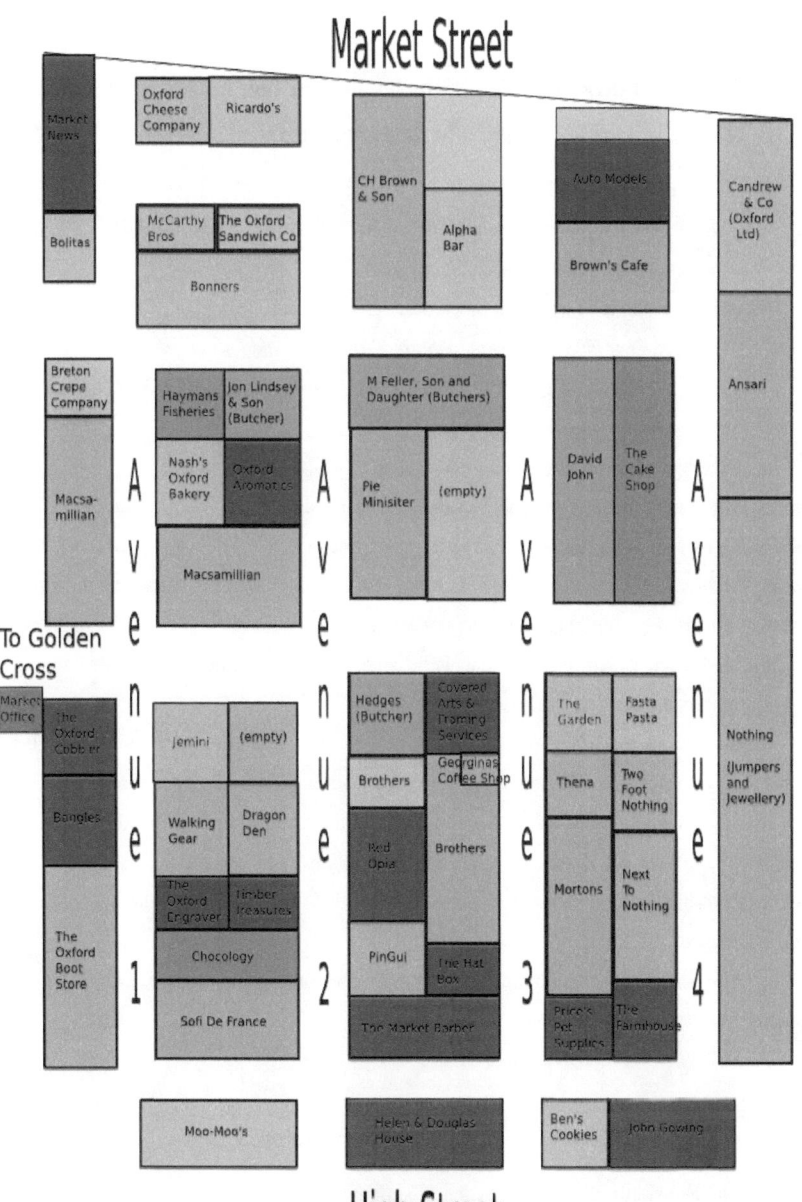

Market News

Oxford Cheese Company

Ricardo's

Bolitas

McCarthy Bros

The Oxford Sandwich Co

Bonners

CH Brown & Son

Alpha Bar

Auto Models

Brown's Cafe

Candrew & Co (Oxford Ltd)

Breton Crepe Company

Haymans Fisheries

Jon Lindsey & Son (Butcher)

M Feller, Son and Daughter (Butchers)

Macsa-millian

Nash's Oxford Bakery

Oxford Aromatics

Pie Minister

(empty)

David John

The Cake Shop

Ansari

Macsamillian

To Golden Cross

Market Office

The Oxford Cobbler

Bangles

The Oxford Boot Store

Jemini

(empty)

Walking Gear

Dragon Den

The Oxford Engraver

Timber Treasures

Chocology

Sofi De France

Hedges (Butcher)

Brothers

Red Opia

PinGui

Covered Arts & Framing Services

Georginas Coffee Shop

Brothers

The Hat Box

The Market Barber

The Garden

Fasta Pasta

Thena

Two Foot Nothing

Mortons

Next To Nothing

Price's Pet Supplies

The Farmhouse

Nothing (Jumpers and Jewellery)

A v e n u e   1

A v e n u e   2

A v e n u e   3

A v e n u e   4

Moo-Moo's

Helen & Douglas House

Ben's Cookies

John Gowing

High Street

The plat is also included in the legal definition for the land which also include three indicators:

- Number of the lot-and-block
- The Subdivision plat's name and/or number
- The country and state information included

Here is an example of a lot-and-block descriptor below:

> Lot 68, Lackawanna State Park 6, located in a part of the southwest of Section 36, Township 8 South, Range 50 West of the Avenue Principal Meridian in Albany Country, State of New York.

When someone accesses the public records to find this legally defined land, they would begin with the Avenue Principal Meridian, as an example, in order to locate it. Then the Township map of Township 8 South would be viewed with Range 50 West. What would follow would be the Section map of Section 36. Next, someone who wants to locate the property would view the quarter-section map in the southwest quadrant. With the plat map, the quarter-section map is connected called the second unit (second parcel subdivided) and related to the name Lackawanna State Park.

According to the Plat Act (765 ILCS 205) when a property owner divides their land into a piece of land that is smaller than five acres, the land must be surveyed and recorded for public record. The exception to this rule is when the land that the property owner divides is less than one acre and does not require any further construction work being done by the city, country and/or township. In some cases, an affidavit is required to show proof that the land does not need to be surveyed.

Since the Plat Act is complicated, this Act does require the assistance of a lawyer and/or county recorder.

Survey Preparation

The legal definitions of land cannot be tampered with by a surveyor, engineer and/or an attorney. Licensed surveyors are trained and qualified to survey any piece of land so that it will pass legal standards. A survey and a survey sketch are the two documents in which a licensed surveyor uses in order to prepare their surveys. The legal definition of the land is in the *survey*. The location and the measurements of the piece of land are in the *survey sketch*. Locations, size, monuments and other distinguishing features of a piece of land that show up in a survey are called a *spot survey*.

In the real world, professional surveyors should always be used to survey a piece of land since legal definitions of land are recorded and affect the title of a property to a landowner.

The legal definitions of land must be recorded and taken down with absolute accuracy and absolute precision, plus much attention to detail. If the information concerning land is incorrect, this can lead to many legal battles and many legal disputes.

Knowledge of various surveys and the uses for them are important as well for real estate licensees to be aware of. Some surveys include warranties and liability, however some do not. For example, an Important Location Certificate (ILC) is not complete survey. ILCs are more cost-effective and only include the monuments, the renovations and the location of the land as all that information connects to the boundaries of the property.

Elevations Measured

This section concerns that property that is owned by landowners that is above the surface of the earth. Elevations come into the equation in regards to condominiums and rights to the air. Rights to the air above land ownership are known as air lots. **Air lots** are determined boundaries that exist above a piece of land.

According to the laws regarding condominiums in all of the states of the United States, a licensed and registered land surveyor must be involved to indicate the elevations of spaces between floors to ceiling as they ascend upwards into the air lots. The vertical boundaries of a unit in a condominium are known as a datum. For example, in a condominium unit, the floor may be 80 feet above the datum and it could have a ceiling that is 89 feet. Usually a separate plat is prepared for the different and the various floors that are contained in a condominium building.

When it comes to the space that is below the ground of a condominium building, such as underground parking available for the condominium owners, this is surveyed in the same way as air lots. The difference is that subsurface space is below the datum rather than above the datum as it is with air lots. Subsurface ground rights do not just have legal definitions that pertain to underground parking. This method is also used for mining, oil extraction and utilities that may be grounded below the surface.

Datum

The definition of a **datum** is a point, line or a surface where elevations can be indicated and/or measured. A licensed and trained surveyor would use a datum to create a legal definition of an air lot concerning a condominium, to record the elevation of a man-made monument such as a highway or to discover subsurface land rights.

In the real world, all large cities use a datum. In Los Angeles, California the datum is called *The Los Angeles City Datum*.

Summary

A legal definition is an authoritative methodology used to determine the exact size of land used for public records, title ownership, to settle legal matters and for court records. There are three methodologies which are used in determining the precise measurements of a piece of land throughout the United States: the metes-and-bound method, the rectangular survey system method and the lot-and-block method (which involves plat maps). The method used to survey land by a licensed and trained land surveyor should be consistent with the previous method that was used for any given piece of land.

With the metes-and-bounds method, which is the oldest method that is in existence that was originally used in the 13 colonies before the United States was formed, this method relies on distance and directions in order to measure the piece of land. Monuments that are a part of the metes-and-bounds are stationary objects which help to determine the boundaries of a piece of land. The actual location in real life of where these monuments are located is more important than how they may have been misreported on a map. As well, with this method, the point of beginning (POB) determines the beginning, as well as the end of how the land surveyor does their work to determine the size of the property.

Most states use the rectangular survey system method. This method uses principal meridians, of which there are 37 principal meridians in the United States not including Hawaii and Puerto Rico and these meridians cover the left to the right of the map that is formed. The closest meridian is not always what determines the boundaries of a property. Legal definitions in this case are permanent and legally binding. Base lines connecting with the principal meridians are the main units of measurements. A given piece of land is determined by one principal meridian and one base line.

Township tiers are formed east and west of the base lines which are six miles apart. Moving north and south, again for six miles, these are known as range strips, or ranges. This results in 36 square mile squares that are called townships.

Correction lines are used to accommodate for the earth being round and the square nature of the rectangular survey system method.

Irregular plots of land are usually surveyed with a mixing of methods in order to create accuracy and precision for the measurements, particularly since these measurements are required for legal definitions. As an example, the metes-and-bounds method and the rectangular survey system method are used in states such as Ohio. For suburban areas of the United States, irregular plots of land are usually measured by both the rectangular survey system method and the lot-and-block method.

Lots, which are indicated by numbers and blocks, which are indicated names and locations are used throughout the United States to mainly survey subdivisions. A plat of the subdivision, which is also a public record, is used by land surveyors to determine the measurements of a suburban area with the lot-and-block method. A plat is a map. Lot-and-blocks also have a Property Identification Number, or (PIN) that is used to indicate property for tax purposes, contracts and surveys that land surveyors use, as well for other legal matters.

Condominium spaces are determined by air lots and their measurements are defined by the datum which is a fixed point that can be used to determine the measurements of air space, such as condominium floors and ceilings that are above the surface of land. This is also known as measuring elevation. Measuring elevation is also done vertically as well. The datum is complemented by benchmarks help to determine to the air lots. Measuring subsurface property such as oil extraction, mining and underground parking lots are also surveyed similar in fashion to air lots.

Quiz

1. Why is it important to have legal definitions of land in the United States? What is its purpose?

2. Name the three methods that are used to determine the legal definitions of land in the United States?

3. What is the oldest method that is used to determine legal land?

4. Describe in detail the first method that is discussed in this chapter?

5. Describe in detail the second method that is discussed in this chapter?

6. When is it necessary to combine the methods used to determine legal land?

7. Describe in detail the third method that is discussed in this chapter?

8. How is space above the ground determined by a land surveyor?

9. How is subsurface property determined by a land surveyor?

10. Describe what subsurface property is as discussed in this chapter?

11. Why would it be important for a lawyer or country reporter to be involved in legal definitions of land?

12. Why is it important for real estate licensees to know about land surveys?

13. How would one measure an irregular piece of land?

14. With the third method discussed in this chapter are the instruments used to determine land public record? *True or False*

15. What is the name of the Act that involves maps as discussed in this chapter? When was it formed?

CHAPTER FOUR: CONTRACTS FOR REAL ESTATE

IN THIS CHAPTER YOU WILL

- Understand what is necessary for a contract to be valid
- Identify the various types of contracts that are used in real estate law
- Present on how contracts can be cancelled and/or discharged legally in real estate law
- Know the difference between unilateral and bilateral, executed and executory, and void, voidable and valid contracts
      Learn how to conduct disciplinary hearings
- Recognize implementation and reason to apply the real estate recovery fund

VOCABULARY TO KNOW

- Assignment
- Bilateral Contract
- Breach of Contract
- Commingling
- Consideration
- Contingency
- Contract
- Conversion
- Counteroffer
- Earnest Money
- Equitable Title
- Executed Contract
- Executory Contract
- Express Contract
- Implied Contract
- Land Contract
- Liquidated Damages
- Novation
- Offer and Acceptance

- Option
- Specific Performance
- Statute of Frauds
- Time is of the Essence
- Unenforceable Contract
- Unilateral Contract
- Valid Contract
- Void Contract
- Voidable Contract

Law of Contracts

The foundation of the real estate business is the law of contracts. Contracts that are created by a seller for a property for the real estate agent to list, as well as the contracts that buyers of property enlist real estate agents for are constantly on-going. An option to buy is a contract and an offer to buy a property is the first part, or first half of the law of contracts as it relates to real estate contract law. Leases for homes and/or apartments, as well as escrows are also considered to be under the law of contracts for real estate. As a real estate professional, one will consistently find themselves involved with the law of contracts in the real estate business. Due to the fact that the law of contracts is so important, it is important to know how contracts work, who are the parties that are involved in a contract and what their obligations are, what are the terms of a real estate contract, as well as how a contract can be broken and what are the consequences of breaking a contract in the real estate business.

Essentially, a **contract** is an agreed upon non-coerced agreement between one or more parties who also fully understand the terms of the contract. If one of the parties involved with the contract did not understand the terms of the contract, the contract can and would be null and void in a court of law. Here is a legal description, or some of the legal components that must be contained within a contract:

- None of the parties involved in a contract can be coerced or forced into the contract
- The act of participation in the contract must be on a voluntary basis

- Similar to how a promissory note works on a more casual basis, contracts are more formal and is a promise and an agreement that is enforceable by law
- The parties involved in signing a contract must be of sound mind, meaning they must be seen as fit by the standards of a court of law to enter into the contract – this way ensuring that the contract is fully understood and no one is being taken advantage of
- There must be something in the contract that is valuable, meaning basically that it would be useless to construct a contract over the value of 2010 U.S. Mint penny, however, if the penny is a 1776 U.S. Mint penny – there would be good reason to construct a contract since the penny would be of value
- The contract must be based on actions that are legal. Contracts that are based on illegal activities are not legally binding

Holders of real estate licenses use contracts in their transactions with buyers, sellers and the public. The United States government law that administrates these transactions is known as contract law.

In the real world, if real estate licensees belong to an association of Realtors® they are required to use forms that are preapproved by the association and preprinted for their contract law transactions. As well, real estate licensees cannot conduct the legal negotiations of a contract without having a license; therefore a lawyer should be consulted.

Implied and Express Contracts

A contract is either implied or expressed, depending on how it is comprised. For an **implied contract**, the conduct and acts of the parties are important. An **express contract** is demonstrated in words and is also known as an *express agreement*. Express contracts can be either written or through the spoken word (or oral). According to the **statute of frauds**, for a contract to be admissible in a court of law, it must be in writing. When contracts are in writing, they are also considered to be enforceable by a court of law, holding all parties involved true to their written words based on the conditions and the terms.

As an example, when a buyer and a seller sign a contract to purchase the seller's home for $800,000, this is an express contract. Using the same example as previously mentioned, when a buyer puts in a bid to purchase the seller's home for $800,000 and there are not any other bids on the home and the seller agrees however there is not anything in writing yet – this is an implied contract.

Contracts between sponsoring brokers and their sponsored licensees must be in writing under The Real Estate Act of 2000.

Unilateral and Bilateral Contracts

Unilateral and bilateral are certain classifications for contracts. Beginning with a unilateral contract, these are contracts where one party agrees to the terms and to the conditions of the contract. In **unilateral contracts**, one party sets up the agreement for a second party to fulfil the terms and conditions of the contract. In this situation, the contract is not legally enforceable upon the second party. If the second party agrees to the contract's terms and conditions, then the first party is legally bound to fulfill the obligations of the contract. An example of a unilateral contract is an option contract. In an option contract, the first party is making an option to purchase a property (in this instance) later. These option contracts come up often for newly built condominiums where new buyers are opting to purchase the home before the condominium is completely built.

A different classification for contracts is **bilateral contracts**. In bilateral contracts, the terms and the conditions of the contract are mutually agreed upon by both parties. In general, the contracts that exist in real estate sales are bilateral contracts. The reason for this is because as an example, the seller is agreeing to sell their home to their buyer and buyer agrees to purchase the home.

Executory and Executed Contracts

If an agreement is formed in a contract or if it is not, it falls under two different categories: executory and executed contracts. When one or more parties in a contract still have obligations to perform under the terms and the conditions of the contract, this is known as an **executory contract**. In real estate, a sales contract when signed is still an executory contract until the sale of the home or property closes. During the transition phase it is an executory contract because one or more parties still needs to fulfill its obligations.

On the other hand, an **executed contract** is when all parties involved have acted according to the terms and the conditions of the contract and the contract's obligations are complete. To make things clear, the word *execute* refers to the action of signing a contract.

Figure 11.1 below shows the process that occurs during a contract which will be discussed further later:

The Formation of a Contract

Before Formed	Formation	After Formed
Elements Involved	Classification	End
Acceptance, Consideration, Determining Purpose, Legal Competency	Implied, Express, Unilateral, Bilateral, Executory, Executed, Enforceable, Unenforceable, Voidable, Void and Valid	Performance, Breach, Damages (Rescission, Performance)

The Ingredients to a Valid Contract

A contract is required to include certain terms and conditions and be based on certain requirements in order for it to be legally binding. This will be discussed in the following.

Offer and Acceptance (Mutual Assent)

With offer and acceptance, as well as mutual assent, there must be an offer made by one party to another party that is mutually agreed upon. This offer also must not be illegal; it must be a legal offer, for the contract to be valid. The *offeror* is the person who makes the offer. The *offeree* is the person who accepts the offer. This entire basic requirement of a contract is known as a *mutual assent*. Each party must completely agree to the terms and to the conditions of the contract in order for it to be valid. In a court of law the terms and the conditions of a contract are looked at to ensure that there was mutual assent involved. The writing of the contract must be clear and easily understand and under the statute of frauds, the contract does require to be in writing, rather than oral.

A **counteroffer** is when changes have been made to the original offer. For example, in buyers' and sellers' market in real estate, an offeror may make a bid for a home that $800,000. Another offeror may make a bid for $820,000. The offeror that made the bid for the home for $800,000 may then place a counteroffer of $860,000 to ensure that they can purchase the home and no one else will out bid them.

Please bear in mind that an offer or a counteroffer can be retracted, withdrawn or taken away at any time as long as there is not acceptance of the offer. In the following, we will discuss acceptance.

Acceptance

In an example such as residential real estate presented just earlier, if the seller of the home agrees to the offer of $860,000 and then signs the contract, this is known as *acceptance* of the contract, or acceptance of the offer. Only when the other party who made the offer, the offeror, is contacted regarding the acceptance of the offer has the process of mutual assent begun.

In the real world, as mentioned earlier in an example, multiple bids on a home (sometimes it could also be commercial real estate or contracts to build condominiums by corporations) can become a legal battleground and requires much care and caution. The obligations of the real estate licensee are to protect their client and to follow the laws of the state regarding licenses.

Consideration

As mentioned at the beginning of this chapter, a penny produced by the U.S. Mint in 2010 would not be of great value; however a penny produced by the United States Mint in 1776 would be of great value. Bringing up this example again is meant to illustrate the importance of value that is a key component in understanding consideration in terms of the law of contract, or contract law. Both parties must equally agree that the considered object, item or agreement is valuable enough to constitute entering into a legally binding contract. Here is another example that follows.

In the example mentioned above of the home that is accepted for offer at the price of $860,000, this home is valuable enough by American standards to enter into a contract and to enter into consideration. Even if that same home was selling for $59,000 in 1981, or even presently in 2016, the sheer exchange of money brings the issue of value into play where consideration is of importance.

The Competence of Legal Parties

The parties that are involved in a contract negotiation, meaning all parties involved in a contract negotiation, need to be considered legally competent (being of sound mind) in order for a contract to be legally binding.

Consent's Reality

Legally, according to the *doctrine of reality of consent*, all parties that enter into a contract must do so willing, without being forced and of their own free will. In a court of law, if a contract is breached, basically meaning broken and will be discussed in more detail later, the argument that can be made in a court of law is that the contract did not have *reality of consent*.

Legal Purpose

As mentioned earlier, a contract must be based on legally binding activities. Contracts that are for illegal purposes are not considered as valid in a court of law.

Contract's Validity

Contracts continue to fall into different categories such as valid, void, voidable or unenforceable. The different types of contracts will be explained below:

- Contracts which are **valid contracts** meet all of the legal requirements to be executed in a court of law
- Contracts which are **void contracts** do not meet all of the legal requirements to be executed in a court law and were not ever legal contracts

- Contracts which are **voidable contracts** may not meet some and/or all of the legal requirements and can be discharged by one or more parties involved
- Contracts which are **unenforceable contracts** meet all of the legal requirements to be executed in a court of law on the surface of the contract, however none of the parties involved can force the other parties involved to execute the necessary obligations contained in the terms and in the conditions of the contract

Contracts and Discharge

When a contract is broken or cancelled by one, both or all parties involved, this is known as a *discharge*. The ideal situation in real estate law is when a contract is completed to its full extent; however a breach or default on one or more parties involved can lead to a termination of the contract and/or discharge.

Contract's Performance

The specific time factors involved with a contract lead to the issues of **time is of the essence** as it relates to contract law. This concept is not too different from paying weekly, bi-weekly or monthly bills for a home or any personal item. Here a very general example will be used.

When you receive your cell phone bill you are required to pay that bill within a certain period of time because you would most likely have an agreement and/or contract with the cell phone company to do so. This example illustrates time is of essence. As well, when you own a home and have a mortgage with the bank (which is basically a contract that they have given you the money to purchase real estate and you will pay back) each payment that you make in time to your mortgage, or even in advance is a strong example of using the good principles of time is of the essence.

If a contract does not say in writing a specific date or time that is important to be mindful of, it should be implied that the actions regarding that contract are carried out within a reasonable amount of time. Next, we will discuss assignment as it relates to the law of contract.

Assignment

Assignment refers to a transfer of the obligations, duties and rights that relate to a contract. The rights of the contract, unless a contract prohibits it, can be assigned to a third party that is also known as an *assignee*. Responsibilities regarding the contract can be *delegated* to the assignee, however the original party involved the contract, or the original signee of the contract would still be held liable if anything were to go wrong according to a court of law.

Novation

The replacement of a new contract for an existing contract is the act known as novation. In employment law, novation is very common. In real estate law, in the situation mentioned earlier where an offeror made a bid of $800,000 on a home were to be accepted verbally, and then renovations were made to the home warranting a more concrete offer of $860,000 as mentioned earlier (such as a pool being put on the property), this would be a simple situation of novation.

Breach of Contract

A breach of contract is when one or more parties involved with a contract terminate the contract and/or violate one its terms and conditions. In this situation from the example just recently used, if the buyer of the home breaches the contract by stating that they no longer want to buy the home for the agreed upon and signed price of $860,000, the seller can then sue the buyer based on **specific performance**, stating that the buyer is under an obligation to perform the duties and to fulfil the duties of the contract. In a lawsuit situation, the seller would receive *liquidated damages*, and the seller may also sue for *compensatory damages* since the time the home was off the market in order to sell due to the offeror's breach of contract requires compensation on the part of the seller.

Statute of Limitations

Every single state within the United States have laws that put a time limit on how long a buyer and/or seller would have to sue regarding any damages resulting from a breach of contract. In general, the statute of limitations for most states tends to be two years, in some states it is three. It is highly recommended that you do your own research into the statute of limitations in the state where you would become a licensed in real estate.

Additional Reasons for a Termination of a Contract

Contracts can also be terminated or discharged for the additional following reasons:

- With a written acceptance by the other party, *partial performance* of the terms and the conditions of a contract
- When one or more of the parties involved in a contract has *substantially performed* all of it duties, however there is still incomplete elements of the contract
- If a house were to burn down after an offeror has signed an agreement for the home, the contract can be terminated based on *impossibility of performance*
- Both parties *mutually agree* to cancel the contract
- If the contract is based on illegal activities, it would then be terminated based on an *operation of law*
- As though the contract had not ever been constructed, *rescission* can cancel a contract

Real Estate's Use for Contracts

Here are most common contracts that are used by managing brokers and brokers:

- Contracts for land or deed contracts
- Agreements for escrow
- Leases
- Buyer agreements and Listing agreements
- Agreements for Options
- Contracts concerning real estate sales

Contract Forms

Due to the fact that so many contracts that are used in real estate occur regularly and are also similar, there are preprinted forms that are used for real estate licensees to fill out in order to ensure all requirements are met for the contract.

Agreements for Buyer and Listing

These contracts are employment contracts. They assist in engaging the work of a real estate licensee with their employment with the buyer or the seller.

Typical Terms in a Sales Real Estate Contracts

The sales contract in real estate is a stated agreement between the buyer and the seller over the purchase of property. Some other terms that may be used for this agreement other than a sales contract are the following: *deposit receipt, earnest money agreement, purchase agreement, contract of purchase and sale,* or *an offer to purchase.* Whatever any real estate licensee calls the sales contract, it is the most important contract that a real estate licensee will ever use for their career.

The Sections of a Sales Contract

The majority of sales contracts are comprised of the following elements:

- The name, intent to purchase and how the purchaser will take the title of the property of the purchaser
- Description of the property for sale, including its address and other key identifiable information as discussed in detail in Chapter 9 and will later be discussed in Chapter 12
- The name, intent to sell and any conditions and terms that the seller has regarding the property on behalf of the seller
- The amount the property is being sold for, including any deposits and earnest money agreements between the buyer and the seller
- The manner in which the property's down payment will be paid for, as an example, in cash

- Information regarding the closing of the contract and the transaction of the sales purchase, including a specific deadline for when the contract will close
- Title details (insurance policy, certificate of title, legal information)
- How other expenses such as fuel costs will be calculated
- A clause that allows for how the contract will be handled if there are any damages to the property
- A right-to-sue provision is also included
- Clauses that are based on contingency, such as lawyer's involvement, financing, etc.
- A settlement agent or a closing agent being appointed
- Instructions on closing or settling the contract
- Impound or escrow account funds transferring
- The transfer of any money regarding extra assessments
- The walk-through, meaning the new owner has the right to inspect the property prior to full possession
- When and where the documents that are required by all parties will be delivered
- The signatures with a date of all of the parties involved. When a property is co-owned or multi-owned, everyone must sign

Additional Inclusions in Contracts

Additional information that is included in a contract consists of the following:

- The provisions of any personal property such as appliances or any lawn equipment

- Any property that must be removed by the seller such as appliances or any lawn equipment

- The transferring of the warranty on items such as furnaces and roofing

- The handling of items such as security systems or cable television devices and whether or not they will be maintained by the buyer and transferred, or returned to the seller

Deposits of Earnest Money

With the customs of real estate, usually a purchaser will give a deposit on the property in good faith that they will indeed purchase the entire property for the agreed upon amount which is of a greater sum of money. This practice is helpful in discouraging buyers from defaulting on contracts.

Escrow Account

Escrow accounts tend to be used primarily to pay for property taxes and for insurance on a home that is a separate account from one used to make mortgage payments. The term **commingling** is when a broker uses their own funds on behalf of the client in order to supplement the deposit amounts of their client. This practice is not encouraged for real estate licensees. Brokers who are sponsored also cannot use the escrow accounts of their clients for their own personal usage – this practice is known as **conversion** and it is illegal. For example, if a real estate licensee uses the money in their client's escrow account to purchase a new Jaguar automobile, this would be seen as conversion and in the contract that the client has with the real estate licensee, the client would then have the right-to-sue through civil litigation and the real estate licensee's actions are also criminally liable as well.

Equitable Title

The purchase of home by a buyer does not conclude with automatic transfer to the title of a home. The deed needs to be delivered and accepted in order for the title of the property to be transferred. As the purchase takes place, the buyer receives **equitable title** of the land involved with the property and the insurance that is involved is also known as equitable title.

Premises Destroyed

If a property that a buyer purchases is destroyed prior to obtaining full possession of that property, the seller is responsible for damage to the property. This is why insurance of property is so vital.

Contingency

Contingency means when there are provisions made in a contract that must be fulfilled in order for the contract to be enforceable in a court of law. The following are some of the contingencies that can exist in real estate law:

- Contingency's specific actions
- Deadlines, due dates and timelines that actions must occur within a contract
- The specific person that is responsible for any expenses that may arise

    The common contingencies in a real estate sales contract are:

- *Mortgage contingency*: the earnest money of the buyer is not spent until the mortgage is secured
- *Inspection contingency*: the property that is going to be purchased may need to be inspected and the fulfillment of the contract is contingent on these inspections
- *Property Sale contingency*: some buyers of a property put the contingency that their own present home needs to sell. This way they would have the funds to purchase the new home
- *Escape Clause*: This clause allows the seller to continue to sell and to market their own property until all of the condition and the terms of the contingencies have been fulfilled

In the situation of contingencies, they are considered and they are categorized as voidable contracts.

Amendments and Addendums

An *amendment* to a contract that has been completed is when it has been changed. Whereas, an *addendums* are any terms and any conditions that are added to an existing contract.

Options

An *option* occurs when an owner of a home, also known as the *optionor*, gives an *optionee* a fixed and a determined price for purchasing their home. In this situation, options are not considered sales contracts, rather they are option agreements once all parties agree to the option and become option contracts once signed and legally binding.

Contracts for Land

A sale of land is also known as a land contract, or a *contract for deed*. With this agreement the seller (or *vendor*) retains the title of the land. The buyer, also known as the *vendee*, is then allowed to use the land once the contract is signed.

Summary

A contract is legally enforceable and therefore can be used in a court of law. If there is a breach of contract, this is usually settled in a court of law.

The classifications of contracts consist of the following: express, unilateral, bilateral, (in terms of the contract's legal enforceability) they are classified as, valid, void, voidable and unenforceable.

Contracts include a time for performance and usually must adhere to deadlines unless not written down. In those instances where contracts do not have dates in place, it is under the assumption of law that a contract will be carried out within a reasonable period of time.

The components of a contract include: competent parties, offer and acceptance, consent, consideration and a legal purpose. In order for a real estate sales contract to be valid, and real sales contracts are most commonly used by real estate licensees, they must be in writing, signed by all parties, as well as not be of an illegal nature.

If the buyer defaults on a contract, the seller have the right to discharge the contract based on situations such as unfulfilled contingencies, and many times can have a right-to-sue depending on the situation that is expressly written into the contract. Some of these unfulfilled contingencies could include an unsecured mortgage, where if the buyer put down earnest money as a deposit on the home, it may be written into the contract for the money to be returned.

The title of the contract is not automatically given in a sales contract. This requires legal intervention.

With an option agreement, an offeror makes and offer to an offeree to buy their home at a fixed price and the offeree agrees. The result is an option contract.

Quiz

1. What kind of law did this chapter cover?

2. What is a definition of a contract?

3. What are the classifications of a contract?

4. What are the enforceable classifications of a contract?

5. Define in detail what are the common contracts that real estate licensees use?

6. What is the most common contract that real estate licensees use?

7. Define in detail the elements to the most common real estate contract?

8. Describe a situation that would make someone want to breach a contract?

9. What are the potential consequences of breaching a contract?

10. What would the court do to resolve disputes between buyers and sellers?

11. What are contingencies in contracts?

12. Describe in detail the different sorts of contingencies of a contract?

13. What is an option agreement?

14. What is an option contract?

15. Describe in detail why it is important for a real estate licensee to know about the details of this chapter, particularly as it concerns potential civil and criminal situations against a real estate licensee?

CHAPTER FIVE: THE ENVIRONMENT AND REAL ESTATE PROFESSIONALS

The Environment and the Real Estate Professional

This chapter focuses on the environmental issues that would affect a real estate professional. Vital federal protection laws regarding the environment will be discussed, learning to distinguish between man-made and natural property hazards will be discussed, and the responsibility of the real estate professional to disclose any environmental hazards as they pertain to real estate will also be discussed.

Residential Lead-Based Paint Hazard Reduction Act

Sick Building Syndrome Underground Storage Tanks (USTs) Urea-Formaldehyde can make a break a deal in real estate. According to the federal law, if a building is sick, this must be disclosed to the potential buyer. The Environmental Protection Act (EPA) which came into effect July 1, 1970 is meant to protect health, welfare, quality of life, as well as property.

The Clean Water Act

With the Clean Water Act, the water qualities standards nationally are set forth by the EPA are determined by the EPA. The Clean Water Act also created a legislative system for the discharge of pollution. Some of the Act's key components contain the following:

- Control programs
- Remove of short-term waste that may create life-threatening situations
- Long-term environmental hazards efforts to permanently resolve

Environmental Assessment

There are four phases or stages of an environmental assessment:

- Phase I: Investigative
- Phase II: Testing
- Phase II: Clean-up
- Phase IV: Management of the site

The Resource Conservation and Recovery Act

The RCRA (also pronounced "rick-rah") gives the EPA the power to contain hazardous waste during its lifecycle. RCRA does not focus on abandoned or historical sites, but active and current sites of real estate.

Safe Drinking Water Act

The SDWA maintains standards for water that are meant to ensure that water is safe for humans to drink and to use.

Property Hazards

Real estate professionals need to keep up-to-date on the latest regarding environmental issues in order to do the best for their clients. An undisclosed property hazard to a potential buyer or a secured buyer could leave the real estate professional liable according to federal law.

Asbestos

The testing procedures that exist to know if asbestos is present in a dwelling are the following:
- Air testing
- Bulk sampling
- Wipe sampling

Carbon Monoxide (CO)

These are the effects of too much carbon monoxide in the blood:

- Dizziness
- Headache
- Nausea
- Drowsiness
- Slower response time
- Unconsciousness
- Death

Most homes require the presence of a CO detector within the home or commercial real estate space.

Chlorofluorocarbons

CFCs deplete the ozone layer. When you add hydrogen to this substance it is known as hydrochloroflourocarbons (HCFCs). Permitting these substances to go into the air can even result in hard prison time.

Electromagnetic Fields

EMFs are invisible. They are created by electrically charged objects such as electric fences as an example.

Soil Contamination

This is a result of paint that is based in lead flaking or chipping.

Residential Lead-Based Paint Hazard Reduction Act

The legislation that exists to disclose these hazards are:

- Total disclosure is legislated by law
- Pamphlets with information
- Homebuyers have 10 days to inspect for lead-based paint issues
- Inclusive language in sales contracts
- Compliance with Title X

Urea-formaldehyde

This substance is a clear chemical that is used for the purposes of manufacturing. The foam insulation of this substance is known as UFFI.

Pests and Naturally Occurring Hazards

Here are some naturally occurring hazards that can happen with real estate:

- Mold
- Pests
- Carpenter ants
- Radon

Summary

This chapter focuses on the environmental issues that would affect a real estate professional. Vital federal protection laws regarding the environment will be discussed, learning to distinguish between man-made and natural property hazards will be discussed, and the responsibility of the real estate professional to disclose any environmental hazards as they pertain to real estate will also be discussed.

Sick Building Syndrome Underground Storage Tanks (USTs) Urea-Formaldehyde can make a break a deal in real estate. According to the federal law, if a building is sick, this must be disclosed to the potential buyer. The Environmental Protection Act (EPA) which came into effect July 1, 1970 is meant to protect health, welfare, quality of life, as well as property.

With the Clean Water Act, the water qualities standards nationally are set forth by the EPA are determined by the EPA.

The RCRA (also pronounced "rick-rah") gives the EPA the power to contain hazardous waste during its lifecycle. RCRA does not focus on abandoned or historical sites, but active and current sites of real estate.

The SDWA maintains standards for water that are meant to ensure that water is safe for humans to drink and to use.

Real estate professionals need to keep up-to-date on the latest regarding environmental issues in order to do the best for their clients. An undisclosed property hazard to a potential buyer or a secured buyer could leave the real estate professional liable according to federal law.

Quiz

16. What is asbestos?

17. What does CO stand for?

18. What are CFCs?

19. What are electromagnetic fields?

20. What is EIS?

21. What is External Environmental Hazards External Obsolescence?

22. Describe in detail what is groundwater as it is described in this chapter?

23. What is mold?

24. What is radon gas?

25. How do environmental issues affect the real estate professional?

26. What are the legal responsibilities concerning disclosure?

27. Name the testing stages for lead?

28. What are the legal Acts mentioned in this chapter that pertain to the environment?

29. Discuss in detail the legal Acts mentioned in this chapter that pertain to the environment?

30. What effect do environmental issues have on a potential buyer's choice of home or commercial real estate?

CHAPTER SIX: TITLES OF RECORD

IN THIS CHAPTER YOU WILL

- Know and understand the different kinds of proof of ownership concerning property
- Identify title issues
- Identify recording and notice of title issues
- Present on the search and process of a title search
- Identify between actual notice and constructive notice

VOCABULARY TO KNOW

- Abstract of Title
- Actual Notice
- Certificate of Title
- Chain of Title
- Constructive Notice
- Marketable Title
- Priority
- Recording
- Subrogation
- Suit to Quiet Title
- Title Insurance
- Title Search

Public Records

In a city or county, the city or county holds the public records for all of the property and/or land that is contained in that area, as discussed previously in Chapter 9. These are vital records that prove the ownership, property liens and notices of encumbrances that would exist on property and/or land. These records guard against any fraudulent activity to protect owners of property and/or land, issues regarding property taxes, creditors and the public in general. Real estate systems that record the records include the following: titles, deeds, and mortgages. Other public records that would contain information regarding marriage, probate, judgements and taxes would also become important when they are linked to real estate records. For the majority of states within the United States, these written documents that are of public record must be located in the same city or county where the property is located. Records of public interest are managed by the following:

- Recorders of deeds
- County clerks
- City clerks
- Clerks of court
- County treasurers
- Collectors

Recording

The process of putting documents forth as public record is known as **recording**. The rules and regulations that are related to recording are set forth by the laws of the state. Basically the rules and regulations must state and do state that any title, deed or document that is related to the ownership of real estate must be kept as public record and accessible to the public. Due to this fact, if someone were interested in a property and wanted to make an offer to the owner of the property, they could do so as long as certain principles and guidelines were in place, such as the owner was not in the process of selling the property through the exclusive rights of a brokerage firm which will be discussed in more detail in Chapter 15. These documents must include certain specific requirements as stated below:

- Grantor's name printed and typed below the signature of the document

- The entire address of the grantee
- Name and address of the person who wrote up the deed
- The Permanent Tax Index Number (this is only required in certain counties)
- The usual address of the property (this is only required in certain counties)
- The completed real estate transfer details
- Proof of payment of the property taxes
- Proof of payment of the municipal transfer taxes

As discussed in Chapter 9, when a piece of land is less than five acres, the Plat Act (765 ILCS 205) applies regarding the recording details for the public records.

In some places in the United States, the department that manages water also must provide public records that the water bills on the property have been paid.

If a public record is not in the language of English, this is still valid between the parties that signed the document, however for the document to be valid for the purposes of the public record; it needs to be translated into English.

Notice

Anyone who has an interest in a particular property can act to try to obtain that property which is known as *giving notice*. There are two different types of notice concerning real estate: *actual notice* and *constructive notice*.

Actual notice: this is also known as *direct knowledge* and the individual giving notice actually knows it. They are directly aware of the ownership concerning the property. They cannot use a constructive notice to justify a claim.

Constructive notice: this is when it can be presumed legally that information regarding giving notice can be obtained. Since the public records exist and the information is common knowledge, it is then up to the individual to give notice based on these public records.

Priority: this means the timeline that is involved regarding the priority of the rights to the property.

Documents that are Unrecorded

There are particular types of liens on property that are not recorded for public record. Property taxes and special assessments are not recorded for public record until these amounts owing are well past due. Franchise taxes and inheritance taxes are mandatory or statutory liens. As with taxes for real estate, as well as special assessments, these taxes are not recorded for public record.

Chain of Title

The record of the property's ownership is the **chain of title**. Starting with the first owner to the current owner, this is what creates the chain of title.

Abstract of Title and Title Search

A **title search** is done to ensure that the chain of title is correct. A summary report of what the title search has found is known as an **abstract of title**.

Marketable Title

At the closing of a sales contract, discussed further in other chapters, the buyer must produce a **marketable title** at the closing of the contract. The following contains what a marketable title must consist of:

- Must not have any errors or any information that would lay any doubt in terms of it being enforceable by law
- Avoid litigation against the buyer of the property
- Legally persuade the purchaser that they could mortgage or sell the property down the road

Proof of Ownership

Evidence that the title is marketable is **proof of ownership**. In many states, a deed alone is not enough to prove proof of ownership.

Certificate of Title

Certificate of title as well is not a complete stamp of approval of ownership. This certificate can be done by an attorney, a title company or a licensed abstractor. A mortgage lender, a buyer or an owner could ask for this certificate.

Attorney's Opinion of Title and Abstract

An attorney's opinion of title and an abstract are used in some states to prove the certificate of title.

Title Insurance

This insurance affects the title that is linked to the property. The following contains the essential elements that are required for a title insurance policy:
- Name of the party being insured
- Description of the real estate as stated by law
- The interest or estate that the policy covers
- Terms and conditions of the policy
- Exceptions schedules, including any defects that may be in the public records

Coverage

A standard **coverage** policy in title insurance usually covers the title as it is stated in the public records.

Title Insurance Policy for the Owner

Standard Policy	Extended Policy	Not included in either policy
-improperly delivered deeds -marital statements that are incorrect -grantors that are incompetent -documents that are forged -errors and/or defects that are found in public records	-includes the standard policy -unrecorded liens that are not aware to the coverage holder -survey and examination -inspection of property	-liens and defects that are listed in the policy -the buyer's knowledge of defects -zoning ordinances and how they change land use

Summary

Public, constructive notice and legal information is given through the use of public records. The system that is in place allows for an organized way for real estate to be transferred. If the public records were not in place it would be next to impossible to transfer real estate between a buyer and a seller. Actual notice is when someone would be personally aware that a property exists, without going through constructive notice which would be the act of going through the public records. If a seller has marketable title, they have title evidence. There is also title insurance that protects the titles of real estate.

There are three different methods that are used for confirming title evidence. They are the following: title insurance policy, certificate of title and attorney's opinion of title and abstract. Title searches are when the chronology of the ownership of a property is conducted.

Quiz

1. What is an abstract of title?
2. What is actual notice?
3. What is a certificate of title?
4. What is a chain of title?
5. What is constructive notice?
6. What is marketable title?
7. What is meant by priority as it relates to public records?
8. Define recording.
9. What is subrogation?
10. What is suit to quiet title?
11. What is title insurance?
12. What are the different types of title insurance?
13. Why is title insurance important?
14. What is a title search?
15. What does a title search do is why is it important?

CHAPTER SEVEN: AGREEMENTS FOR BROKERAGE

IN THIS CHAPTER YOU WILL

- Understand buyer representation agreements
- Understand employment contracts that are used between buyers and sellers to hire a real estate professional
- Understand the listing agreements and the purpose for each one
- Understand a buyer agency agreement and its purpose
- The terms and the conditions commonly found in a brokerage agreement
- Understand a rental finding service agreement and its purpose
- The regulations for dealing with earnest money

VOCABULARY TO KNOW

- Buyer Agency Agreement
- Commingling
- Conversion
- Escrow Moneys
- Escrow Account
- Exclusive Agency Agreement
- Exclusive Right to Sell
- Listing Agreement
- Minimum Services
- Multiple Listing Service
- Net Listing
- Open Listing
- Procuring Cause
- Rental Finding Service

Agreements for Brokerage

The buyers and the sellers of property hire real estate professionals using buyer brokerage agreements or listing agreements. These agreements are also called buyer representation agreements. These agreements are also known to be **employment contracts**. The contracts allow the real estate professional to act on behalf of the buyer and/or seller. This chapter will focus on the various types of brokerage agreements and the obligations of a broker when dealing with earnest money.

Agreements for Listing

Listing agreements occur between the seller of a property and a real estate agent in order to set out the terms and conditions involved for the real estate agent to sell the seller's property. Listing agreements are also called **service provision contracts**, or service provision agreements. Listing agreements come in various forms and they basically set out the terms and the conditions that are required for the broker, or real estate agent, to fulfill their obligations in order to sell the property of the seller at a commissioned rate of compensation. A typical listing agreement would consist of the following:

- **List price**
- The contractually agreed upon rate of **commission**
- A **definite termination date** of the agreement, as well as its **duration**
- The real estate agent and the seller's **names**
- **Signatures** of both the real estate agent and the seller
- The obligations and **duties** of the listing broker
- Unless a different type of agency working relationship is agreed to, the **designated agent** would also be included in the employment contract
- In some states of the United States, **dual agency** is also required as it relates to disclosure of information and documents

Selling Agreement and Exclusive Rights

When a real estate agent has an exclusive right to sell a seller's property, this is known as an **exclusive right to sell agreement**. This type of employment contract encourages the broker/real estate agent to work very hard at selling the seller's property. Under this contract, the broker will be paid regardless of who sells the property. It could be the seller himself or herself who sells the property and the broker/real estate agent would still be paid their commission on the sale price. An exclusive right to sell agreement is an enforceable contract and **must be in writing**.

Agreements of Exclusive Agency

This agreement is similar to the exclusive right to sell agreement, however in this instance; the broker/real estate agent also has the exclusive right to **represent the seller** in selling their property. This is known as **exclusive agency**. The broker will receive their commission, unless the seller sells the property himself or herself to a person or persons who are exempted in the listing agreement. As well, the broker/real estate agent will also not be compensated if any other **real estate agent** or **real estate agency** sells the property on behalf of the seller. Again these employment contracts are enforceable and they must be in writing.

Agreements of Open Listing

With an **open listing agreement**, the word implies its meaning. The seller is open to sell his or her property to as many brokers/real estate agents as they choose to do so. There are not any exclusive rights that any particular or many real estate agents would have over the sale of the property on behalf of the seller. The broker/real estate agent only secures their commission if they are the **procuring cause**, or reason why the sale of the property took place. The terms and the conditions in an open listing agreement are clearly put in writing, however a real estate agent/broker would only receive their commission if they meet the sale price requirements of the seller and other terms and conditions set forth in the open listing agreement.

As an added note, with some of the zoning laws in some places in the United States, there would be a limit on the number of signs that can be placed by a real estate agent/broker on the property of the seller.

Net Listings

A **net listing** is not a true listing at all. What a net listing is describes a method of compensation that a real estate agent and/or broker receive in an employment contract. Net listings are illegal in most states of the United States. A real estate agent/broker could be subject to charges of fraud in many states because the seller did not understand the actual value of their property due to the net listing.

Listing Agreements and Provisions

The terms in a listing agreement are subject to negotiation. The first thing that tends to be clarified in a listing agreement is its category (exclusive rights, open listing, exclusive agency, etc.). The usual listing agreement consists of the following elements within the contract:

Contract's Parties

The parties who are involved with a contract must be clearly and expressly written down:
- The people that have a share in the ownership of the property that is listed must be clearly and expressly written done in order for it to enforceable in a court of law
- The company name of the brokerage, the broker/real estate agent that is employed, the real estate agent that is listing the property, should all be clearly and expressly named in the listing agreement employment contract
- Also of importance would be an indication in the employment contract of whether or not the seller has hired on another or an additional brokerage company

Property's Description

Similar as to what was discussed in Chapter 9 regarding the importance for a real estate agent to understand the legal definition of land, as well as in Chapter 12 the importance of understanding contracts used in real estate law, the property's description is also important when it comes to the employment contracts that are used between sellers and brokers. The street address, descriptors that clearly indicate where the property is located such as the town and/or state, are all important information to include in the listing agreement.

Sale Price of the Home

The price that the property is listing for is the **seller's responsibility**. A broker can make a suggestion to the seller based on the going rate of other properties in the area and what other neighbors who have sold have asked for with their properties in terms of selling the property, however ultimately the asking price of a property is the seller's responsibility. The seller knows their property best and they may have made substantial upgrades to their property that would up sell the property higher in value compared to other homes in the neighborhood. The asking price is the seller's responsibility.

Contract Term

An employment contract must have an expiration date. Typically these listing agreements have an expiration date of 90 to 120 days which is known as the **term contract**. Midnight is the time that is involved with the end time of a term contract.

Broker's Fees Payments

The rate of commission or flat fee that is agreed upon between the seller and the broker/real estate agent must be negotiated. It is a violation of United States anti-trust laws to give a fixed price on the payment involved in broker's fees. Nor should your fee be discussed with competing brokerage firms. The commission may be a percentage of the asking price or whatever would be the final sale price of the property depending if the property under sells or over sells regarding to the asking price.

Additional Elements to a Listing Agreement

Here are some optional, but recommended, additions to a listing agreement:
- **Cooperation with other brokers**
- **Permission to advertise**
- **Disclosure**
- **Personal Property or lease agreement**

Clauses which are Optional

Here are some optional clauses that may be included in a listing agreement:
- **Proof of ownership**
- **Indemnification clause**: means the seller and broker will not sue each other
- **Conflicts of Interest**
- A clause stating that the seller will not hire another broker
- **Seller financing agreement**: a promissory note that includes the terms of the loan involved with the property for sale
- A clause stating that the seller will not cash the cheque of the earnest money given to him or her from the buyer

Multiple Listing Service

The Multiple Listing Service, or MLS, is an online service that lists properties that are for sale and their asking prices. It is common that the MLS is used by potential purchasers of property to seek out a particular area they want to live in, as well as a particular price of a home that is within their budget, plus the size and the dimensions of the home that they are looking for through the MLS service.

Listing Agreement Revoked

It is up to the seller, they can retract or they can revoke a listing agreement and/or an employment contract between a seller and a broker/real estate agent at any given time of the contract. The good thing for the broker in this case is that if this contract is revoked prior to the expiration of the contract's term, this is considered to be a breach of contract and does in fact violate the rights of the broker/real estate agent. The broker can in a court of law, or through an out of court settlement, request for compensatory damages due to the breach of contract. However, if the revocation of the listing agreement is for **cause**, the seller would not be at any risk of compensatory damages to the broker for cancelling the contract.

Agreements of Buyer Agency

Agreements between the buyer and the broker/real estate agent are known as **buyer brokerage agreements**. These agreements are also known as a buyer representation agreement, a buyer agency agreement, a buyer listing or a buyer broker contract as well. These are written employment contracts and again enforceable by law. There are two typical forms for these agreements: exclusive and non-exclusive (open) agreements.

The basic requirements of these agreements include:

- Compensation agreement
- Duration
- Names of all parties involved
- Signatures of all parties involved
- Obligations and duties of the broker/real estate agent

In a different document, the **designated agent** may be named. If there is **dual agency** involved in the buyer agreement, disclosure may also be included in the employment contract, or in a separate document.

Exclusive Rights in a Buyer Agency Agreement

Similar to how the exclusive rights of a seller agreement works, the exclusive rights in a buyer agreement works the same way. When a real estate agent has an exclusive right to buy property for a buyer, this is known as an **exclusive right to buy agreement**. This type of employment contract encourages the broker/real estate agent to work very hard to purchase the property for the buyer. Under this contract, the broker will be paid regardless of who sells the property. It could be the buyer himself or herself who buys the property and the broker/real estate agent would still be paid their commission on the sale price. An exclusive right to buy agreement is an enforceable contract and **must be in writing**.

Open Buyer Agency or Non-Exclusive Rights

This agreement is similar to the exclusive right to buy agreement, however in this instance; the broker/real estate agent also has the exclusive right to **represent the buyer** in purchasing other property. This is known as **non-exclusive rights**. The broker will receive their commission, unless the buyer purchases property himself or herself to a person or persons who are exempted in the listing agreement. As well, the broker/real estate agent will also not be compensated if any other **real estate agent** or **real estate agency** works to buy property on behalf of the buyer. Again these employment contracts are enforceable and they must be in writing.

With an **open buyer agency**, the word implies its meaning. The buyer is open to buy his or her property through as many brokers/real estate agents as they choose to do so. There are not any exclusive rights that any particular or many real estate agents would have over the sale of the property on behalf of the buyer. The broker/real estate agent only secures their commission if they are the **procuring cause**, or reason why the sale of the property took place as it works on the sales end of these contracts as well. The terms and the conditions in open buyer agency are clearly put in writing; however a real estate agent/broker would only receive their commission if they meet the sale price requirements of the buyer and other terms and conditions set forth in the open buyer agency.

In Practice

Relationships are built between the sponsoring broker and the seller and the buyer through listing agreements. For real estate agents and real estate professionals this would mean that as they conduct their business, it is the sponsoring broker, or the brokerage that is truly in the limelight regarding the sales or the purchases of a home, rather than the broker/real estate agent himself or herself.

Agreements that are Exclusive

All of these agreements must be in writing in order to be enforceable in a court of law. The minimum requirements of the duties of a real estate broker include the following:

- Accept and then present to the client any offers from offerors to buy or sell property, as well as leasing property
- Assist the client with any offers or counteroffers by the offerors in terms of property negotiations and their contingencies
- Respond to the questions of the clients in a timely manner

If these minimum requirements are not included in the employment contract, the contract then becomes non-exclusive.

Requirements that are General

If employment contracts or listing agreements do not include a clause for automatic expiration, they are automatically void and not enforceable by law. The following includes some other requirements that are general to employment contracts and/or listing agreements:

Commission for Work Done

Each contract that is writing must include the commission that is to be paid out to the real estate agent/broker. This commission as mentioned previously can either be a percentage of the final sale of the property or a flat fee.

Fair Housing

The **fair housing** clause prohibits the prevention of sale of a home based on discriminatory practices. A buyer or seller of a home cannot be discriminated against based on their race, color, religion, sexual orientation, disability, etc. Please also bear in mind that regardless of whether or not a broker/real estate agent is involved in the selling or buying of a home, **discrimination is against the law**.

Agreements Based on Future Brokerage

A real estate agent/broker can have a conversation with a buyer and/or seller of property, even if they are under an exclusive agreement with another brokerage firm, bearing in mind the following conditions:

- The potential client initiates the conversation based on future brokerage
- The current real estate agent or brokerage does respond within 10 days regarding the contract between their client and their firm

Protection for the Broker

A **broker protection clause** in the employment contract ensures that the broker/real estate agent will receive their commission as long as all of the conditions and the terms of the employment contract were met by the expiration date of the contract.

Contacting Permission

The employment contract also states stipulations concerning how and in what is the best way or fashion to contact the client.

Finding Service for Rentals

In many states throughout the United States there is a **Rental Finding Service**. These services help people to find rental property for a fee. They operate under some of the following conditions:

- Residential rental real estate units, or

- Leasing of residential rental real estate property

The various types of companies that exist within the United States such as: limited partnership, partnership, Limited Liability Company or corporation must be licensed in order to run a rental finding service under the Real Estate License Act of that particular state in question, unless they are excluded.

Rental Units and their Contracts

Since the individuals that use rental finding services pay a fee, they enter into a written contract with the company that is offering to help them to find a rental property to lease. The following are the components of the **rental finding service contracts**:
- The contract's terms
- The fee for the services of the rental finding contract
- Any statements referring to a refund or a non-refund for fees paid by the client
- The kind of rental unit that is wanted, the area or location of the unit, and the amount of rent that the client wishes to pay
- In detail, a statement in writing by the rental finding services of the services that they will provide
- A clause in the contract that if details regarding rental units are not up-to-date, the contract is then void and null

- A noted clause that details regarding rental units may be as old as two days to protect the rental finding service
- A refund clause that also states when that refund will be returned

Disclosure of Rental Agreement Information

Here is information on what needs to be disclosed to a client by a rental finding service:
- Name, address and telephone number, also email address if needed
- Details regarding the description of the rental
- Rent amount
- Amount of security deposit
- Information regarding utilities
- The start of the lease and the end of the lease
- The source of the rental details must be included, for example by owner or by an agent
- Any other pertinent details

Dealing with Earnest Money

A home is probably the single most expensive thing that an American or an American family will ever purchase in their lifetime. It is of great importance that a real estate agent and/or broker handle the money in which they are given concerning the sale or purchase of a home with great caution and with great care. Failure to do so is a violation of the law and can lead to both civil and criminal consequences in a court of law.

Earnest money deposits happen when a buyer of a home is not considering to purchase the home, however would like to keep the home in trust so-to-speak in case they decide to purchase the home. It is up to the buyer's broker to keep this money safe and to not squander it. It could be that it is the **listing broker** that would actually put these funds of earnest money into an escrow account. Bear in mind that nothing else can be done with earnest money other than to put those funds into an escrow account.

The Basics of an Escrow Account

In most states throughout the United States, escrow accounts in real estate must be in a **federally-insured** deposit account. This account must be different from any other personal and/or business bank accounts. Sponsoring brokers can manage more than one escrow account. Next, we will discuss how certain elements that would come into play with these escrow accounts should be handled by a broker:

- **Interest**: escrow accounts should not be producing any interest accrued
- **Demand account**: the account holder can access the funds at any given time
- **Timing of deposit**: earnest money and money in an escrow account must be immediately given to their sponsoring broker
- **Notification**: the sponsoring broker needs to contact all of the parties involved concerning the escrow account in writing. This way it makes it legally enforceable
- **Maintenance and Disbursement**: the broker must manage the funds until the termination of the employment contract and release the funds no later than the next business day after the termination of the listing agreement

Conversion and Commingling

It is very important that a real estate agent and/or broker does not even put one penny into an escrow account to supplement the funds of their client. If this is done, that is known to be **commingling** and is punishable by law.

Conversion is when a real estate agent and/or broker were to use the funds in an escrow account for their own personal use or for the expenses of a brokerage firm. This too is punishable by law.

Earnest Money Disputes

In order to avoid any problems with the earnest money that comes into play in buying or selling real estate, this should be stated in the purchase agreement. In the event that problems do occur, the person who gave the earnest money would be entitled to **liquidated damages** in a court of law. The damages if awarded would take place as civil litigation in a court of law, meaning the earnest money giver would be suing the seller and/or the real estate agent and/or broker, and/or the brokerage firm.

Keeping of Records

In most states throughout the United States, a bookkeeper must be present in a brokerage firm in order to keep track of the escrow accounts that temporarily come into their possession. The basic requirements for maintaining these records include the following:

- A **journal** which indicates the timeline of the funds coming in
- A **ledger** which indicates the disbursement and receipt of the funds for the escrow accounts
- A **monthly reconciliation statement** that must be up-to-date 10 days after the statements from the bank, as well as maintained for five years for record keeping
- A master escrow account log that indicates the bank account numbers, earnest money possessors and addresses of the bank where the escrow funds are held

The duties of the record keeping could be given to a certified public accountant, a bookkeeper, a managing broker or any other person who can manage the job well by the brokerage firm.

Maintenance Records

Records for escrow accounts must be retained for five years. Records that are from the past two years must be located at the brokerage firm and upon request by brokerage firm personnel these records must be produced within 24 hours. Any records that are more than two years old can be stored outside or offsite of the brokerage firm. If these records need to be inspected, they must be made available within 30 days of the request.

Records that are Electronic

The records that are used for escrow accounts can either be done in hard copy or electronically. There must be backups of the records done at least every 60 days and the electronic copies can be stored both onsite and offsite of the brokerage firm.

Summary

A listing agreement is an employment contract between the buyer and the brokerage firm. These contracts often have non-exclusive or exclusive rights. Exclusive agreements contain a broker protection clause that can hold the buyer and/or seller liable for breach of the employment contract. All contracts must be in writing to be enforceable by law.

An exclusive listing right to sell agreement between a seller and a broker or brokerage firm gives that broker the exclusive right to sell the seller's property. An open listing agreement puts the seller in a position where they are not obligated to commit to any one particular broker in order to sell their home. A non-exclusive listing agreement still gives some rights to a brokerage firm; however the seller has the choice to hire on another brokerage firm. Net listings are illegal and prohibited by law.

When a buyer enlists a brokerage firm, it is known as a buyer brokerage agreement. The same structures that are used in selling a home also apply to buying a home. As with selling a home, employment contracts between buyers and brokerage firms are known as exclusive, non-exclusive and open as well and follow the same terms and the same conditions as those for sellers of homes, with the exceptions that that the buyer is looking to purchase a home, rather than to sell a home.

Brokers need to be very careful and very careful in handling earnest money given to them in a purchase of a home. This earnest money is handled with great care legally, since commingling or conversion of these funds can lead to both civil and criminal consequences. The earnest money is put into an escrow account and there is also record keeping on the part of the brokerage firm to ensure that the money is kept safe.

Rental Finding Services are run by companies who entering into rental listing agreements with clients who are looking to lease homes. These contracts follow certain stipulations such as including the amount of rent the client wants to pay, information regarding utilities and the location of the rental unit as well as other pertinent details. A client would pay a fee to the companies that run rental finding services.

Quiz

1. What exactly are the agreements of brokerage?

2. What exactly are the agreements for listing?

3. Describe in detail what is the nature of exclusive rights are as discussed in this chapter?

4. Describe in detail what is the nature of non-exclusive rights as discussed in this chapter?

5. Describe in detail what is the nature of open rights as described in this chapter?

6. What is called the agreements between buyers and brokerage firms?

7. Describe the detail what is the nature of exclusive rights as it relates to buyers agreements?

8. Describe in detail what is the nature of non-exclusive rights as it relates to buyers agreements?

9. Describe in detail what is the nature of open rights as it relates to buyers agreements?

10. What is meant by earnest money?

11. What is an escrow account?

12. What is commingling?

13. What is conversion?

14. Describe in detail what is involved in a Rental Finding Service as discussed in this chapter?

15. Describe in detail how brokerage firms keep their records (as well as electronic) for handling escrow accounts?

CHAPTER EIGHT: PRINCIPLES OF REAL ESTATE FINANCING

- Mortgagee
- Mortgagor
- Negotiable Instrument
- Non-judicial Foreclosure
- Novation
- Prepayment Penalty
- Promissory Note
- Release Deed
- Satisfaction of Mortgage
- Sheriff's Deed
- Sheriff's Sale
- Statutory Right of Redemption
- Statutory Right of Reinstatement
- Strict Foreclosure
- Theory
- Title Theory
- Usury

Financing Real Estate

Real estate is bought with money. Since real estate is so expensive, most homes are purchased with the help of a bank, money that is borrowed from the bank also known as **financing**. The financing that is used for a home is also known as getting a **mortgage** for a home. The financial banking industry that exists currently for helping people and real estate developers to finance the purchase of property is a huge and a successful market servicing many people. A client also being able to get the money through financing to purchase a property is of paramount importance. Without the funds to purchase a property, a client or company would be unable to purchase the home at all, leaving the real estate professional out of work. Understanding how this area works in regards to real estate is necessary and an important element of the real estate agent's job.

In Chapter 15 and Chapter 16 of this book, these chapters will help you to understand how to help the buyer or seller to make the important decisions regarding where to get their financing to purchase a home. It is vital that a real estate professional is familiar with the variety of financing options that are available to a potential client. This will help them to have more options in regards to being preapproved for a home so their offers are more solid in order to acquire real estate.

Debt and Security

One of the base rules of property law is that no one can transfer or have more than they actually own. The same is true for mortgages as well. The person who has a mortgage on a property must be able to pay the principle balance of that mortgage. The person who is a leaseholder or a sublease holder must be able to pay the interest that accrues on that lease. Someone who owns a condominium apartment can mortgage the condominium fee of that apartment.

Mortgage Loans

The relationship between a debtor and a creditor is a **mortgage** relationship. The debtor is the person who is borrowing the money and the creditor is the lender of the money in order for the debtor to eventually pay off the loan in order to own the property in full. This latter example is the ideal situation. The debtor also gives up some collateral in order to own their property, such as being willing to hand over their property back to the bank if they are unable to pay for the mortgage.

Promissory Notes

A **promissory note** that is also known as a **financing instrument** and/or a **note**, is when the **mortgagee** or **borrower** is giving a personal promise to their **creditor** to repay the debt based on certain terms and conditions. The promissory note states all of the assets that the mortgagee has that can be seized by **secured creditors**. The mortgagor would give one or more notes or financial instruments to the amount of the debt to the mortgagee.

A promissory note that is used by the borrower, also known as the maker or payer is indeed a legally binding contract. It states the debt amount, as well as the time in which under the terms and conditions the debt should be paid. A promissory note is not necessarily linked with a deed of trust or a mortgage. It is basically a debt instrument. A debt instrument without any concrete collateral is known as an unsecured note. The lender or financial institution that holds the financial instrument is known as the payee and has the authority to transfer get payment to a third party when they sign the promissory note over to a third party.

Fee for Loan Origination

Loan origination is the procedure involved of a mortgage application. A fee is charged for this service. It is also known as a **loan origination fee**. The government of the United States handles the fee as discount points against the costs associated with borrowing money. The discount points equate to 1% of the amount of the loan and are included in interest that is prepaid at the closing of the deal.

Deed of Trust or Mortgage Document

The **deed of trust** or **mortgage document** confirms the property's security for the debt (or mortgage) to a **lender**. These documents need to be signed by all parties and in writing in order to be legally binding.

Deed of Trust

In some circumstances the borrowers' may prefer to have a **three-party instrument** also known as a **deed of trust**, or a **trust deed**, instead of a mortgage. This document gives **legal title** to the property without ownership of the property. The third party is known as the **trustee**. They hold the rights to the title on behalf of the lender also known as the beneficiary. The promissory note is held by the beneficiary. If the trustor, or borrower, does not pay the debt this is a protection of the terms and the conditions written out in the **deed**.

Prepayment

Mortgage loans are usually paid either bi-weekly or monthly in parcels of money to the lender, also known as **installments**. This is usually done over a very long period of time since the price of real estate tends to be expensive. The **interest** that is accrued is calculated by lenders to determine how much money they can profit on by lending the mortgage to the mortgagee. There are penalties if a **mortgage payment** is either late or in default.

Trustor and Duties of the Mortgagor

There are certain obligations that the borrower of a deed of trust and/or mortgage must abide by. These obligations include payment of the mortgage to the lender, adhering to the terms and the conditions of the promissory note, or note, paying the real estate taxes as well as the general property taxes, insuring the home against any problems that may occur, committing to the upkeep of the home so it remains in good standards. Failure to adhere to these terms and conditions set forth between the borrower and the lender can create a default in the duties of the borrower. The borrower is given a 30 day grace period in writing if they are not meeting their duties in order to rectify the situation. If the situation is not rectified then the lender can take possession of the collateral concerning the borrowing relationship and the borrowing relationship could potentially end without further negotiations.

Provisions for Default

There is also an **acceleration clause** that is included in a deed of trust or a mortgage that helps the lender in the event of **foreclosure**. The lender would then have the rights, if the borrower defaults on their obligations, to foreclose on the property. This basically means that the property is no longer owned by the mortgagor. The lender would then be advancing, also known as accelerating, the end of the debt that is owed.

Mortgage's Assignment

A promissory note may be given or transferred to a third-party without the terms and the conditions and/or provisions of the sales contract being changed to, for example, another **mortgage company** or to an **investor**. The note needs to be endorsed.

Mortgage Lien's Release

Here is most homeowner's dream come true: all of the mortgage loan payments have been paid in full and the mortgagor will want the **public record** to indicate that the debt has been fully satisfied and the debt has been fully paid. There is a defeasance clause in the majority of **mortgage documents** that will **discharge a borrower** from any further payments of their debt since the debt is complete. This also helps to remove a **lien**, also known as a **mortgage lien**, on a given property. This is done by what is known as a **recorded assignment** and must be done by an **assignee** or a **mortgagee**.

When a debt has been paid in full, the **beneficiary** must express in writing to the trustee to transfer the property to the **grantor**. It is the trustee that delivers a deed that is released, also known as a **deed of reconveyance** to the **trustor**. The same rights and powers that the **trustee** had of the deed of trust also apply to the **release deed**. These documents should also be legally noted in the public records. As mentioned in a previous chapter, these documents of public record, as mentioned in Chapter 13, are usually located in the township or county where the property exists.

If all this necessary steps are not done within one month of the paid in full status of a property there will be a penalty of $200 to the **mortgagor**. These laws also protect the owner because it is vital that these records be publically accessible.

Insurance Reserves and Taxes

Borrowers are required to have funds on reserve in order to meet the requirements for owning property. This helps to protect the property against any liability. It protects against situations such as unpaid real estate taxes and/or property taxes, as well as to ensure that there are available funds for property insurance and to account for an insurance premium reserve. Escrow accounts usually account for creating reserve funds for a property owner.

Rent Assignments

When it comes to real estate that involves **rental property**, the mortgagee can give for **rents to be assigned** to the lender in the event of the mortgagor's default. This may be included in the deed of trust or the mortgage. It can also be in a different document. It needs to clearly indicate that the rents are being **assigned** as collateral for the property's debt.

Mortgage and Deed of Trust Priorities

Other liens and the priority of mortgages are calculated and prioritized in the order they have been recorded. A deed of trust or mortgage that does not have a mortgage lien is the first deed of trust or **first mortgage**. If the mortgagor creates an additional loan for more funds, the new loan then becomes the **second mortgage** or deed of trust, this is also known as a **junior lien** as it is recorded. The **second lien** has previous claim to the value of the land that is pledged as security. There are higher interest rates involved with these transactions.

Returned Checks and Fees

Land contracts can also be the means in which real estate is bought as discussed in Chapter 11. There are usually certain financial reasons why real estate is sold through a contract. As an example, through **mortgage financing** that may not be accessible to the borrower, or high rates of interest may not be feasible to the borrower, or the person buying the property does not have enough of a **down payment** in order to come up with the **mortgage loan** for the selling price of the property.

A **land contract** is also known as an **installment contract** or a **contract for deed**. The buyer, also known as the **vendee** enters a contract to make a monthly loan payment and a down payment that is inclusive of the principal and the interest that goes direct to the seller of the property. This payment includes the insurance reserves and the real estate tax as well. The seller in this case is known as the **vendor** and they retain the **legal title** to the real estate throughout the contract term and the vendee is given a **granted equitable title** and **possession**. When this contract is finished or at the completion of the **loan term**, the seller delivers the **clear title** of the land to the vendee. If the seller does not give the clear title to the buyer, the vendee can file a lien on the property. The seller can also evict the buyer if the vendee is in default or fails to make the payments on the property.

These contracts can happen with commercial and/or residential property and take place usually with acreage and farmland purchases. The seller is usually the **primary lender**, or sometimes the seller takes on a secondary role.

Foreclosure Methods

There three basic types of foreclosure proceedings are **strict foreclosure, judicial** and **nonjudicial**. The terms and the conditions for each of these are different from each state to state within the United States. In terms of **nonjudicial foreclosure**, some states permit nonjudicial foreclosure processes to be used with the security instrument includes a power-of-sale clause. With this process, there is not any court action or legal action that is required.

With **judicial foreclosure**, the property is permitted to be sold through court order and after the mortgagee or borrower has provided sufficient public notification. When a **mortgagee** defaults, the lender can then accelerate the amount owing remaining principal of the debt, including any administrative costs, penalties and interest. The attorney for the lender can then file a lawsuit to foreclose the lien. There is a court proceeding and after a presentation of the facts and the circumstances, the property is then sentenced to be sold. There is a public sale where the property is held and advertised and the real estate is given to the buyer who is willing to purchase it at the highest price.

Sole owner or **joint tenant**, or **tenant by the entirety**, sells or leases by statute, **mortgage foreclosures** can happen only through a court proceeding. In different states this is known as the Mortgage Foreclosure Law (735 ILCS 5/) and the **term mortgage** is inclusive.

Strict Foreclosure

Judicial foreclosure is more common; however sometimes in some states a lender receives a mortgaged property through a **strict foreclosure** procedure. With this procedure, appropriate notice is given to the defaulted borrower. After this papers are then served and recorded and the court states a deadline where the balance of the debt must be paid in full. If the borrower or mortgagee does not pay the loan by the deadline then the court gives full title of the property to the lender. There is not any sale of the property that takes place in this procedure.

Deeds of Trust

The following are examples of deeds of trust and what they must contain:

- **Installment contracts** that must be paid over a period of five years (the amount that is not paid must be less than 80% of the actual price)
- **Beneficial interest** in **land trusts** that are used for **security lenders** as certain **collateral assignments**
- **Mortgage instruments** that are traditional

Deed in Lieu of Foreclosure

Foreclosure does have other alternatives such as a lender could accept a **deed in lieu of foreclosure** from the mortgagee. This is known as a **friendly mutual agreement** and does not involve a lawsuit. The borrower would take the real estate on condition to all of the liens. With foreclosure, all **junior liens** are deeds in lieu of foreclosure and the lender would not have the right to pertain to FHA or private **mortgage insurance** or VA guarantees. A deed in lieu of foreclosure is considered a hit to the borrower's credit score.

Government Programs

There are **financial programs** to make real estate affordable such as **the Making Home Affordable** (MHA) program, which is a part of the government helping borrowers, as well as the **Home Affordable Modification Program** (RAMP), plus the **Home Affordable Refinance Program** (HARP). With these programs which are done on a voluntary basis, not all of the lenders participate. With a program such as RAMP as an example, not more than 31% of the monthly pretax income of the borrower is used to calculate the increase term up to 40 years, reduce the principal of the loan and to determine the interest rate.

Redemption

There are moments when a borrower who has defaulted on their mortgage can have a chance for **redemption** in order to receive the **equitable right of redemption**. Before foreclosure, but after default, the borrower would pay the lender the amount in default, including the costs of the debt that will be reinstated for regular payments that begin again. Sometimes the person who redeems must repay the accelerated loan amount in full. In some states in the United States the defaulted borrower has a period of time to redeem their real estate after it has gone for sale, usually this time period could be one full calendar year in length. The borrower has a **legal right of redemption**.

Summary

Real estate is bought with money. Since real estate is so expensive, most homes are purchased with the help of a bank, money that is borrowed from the bank also known as financing. The financing that is used for a home is also known as getting a mortgage for a home. The financial banking industry that exists currently for helping people and real estate developers to finance the purchase of property is a huge and a successful market servicing many people. A client also being able to get the money through financing to purchase a property is of paramount importance. Without the funds to purchase a property, a client or company would be unable to purchase the home at all, leaving the real estate professional out of work. Understanding how this area works in regards to real estate is necessary and an important element of the real estate agent's job.

The relationship between a debtor and a creditor is a mortgage relationship. The debtor is the person who is borrowing the money and the creditor is the lender of the money in order for the debtor to eventually pay off the loan in order to own the property in full. This latter example is the ideal situation. The debtor also gives up some collateral in order to own their property, such as being willing to hand over their property back to the bank if they are unable to pay for the mortgage.

A promissory note that is also known as a financing instrument and/or a note, is when the mortgagee or borrower is giving a personal promise to their creditor to repay the debt based on certain terms and conditions. The promissory note states all of the assets that the mortgagee has that can be seized by secured creditors. The mortgagor would give one or more notes or financial instruments to the amount of the debt to the mortgagee.

A promissory note that is used by the borrower, also known as the maker or payer is indeed a legally binding contract. It states the debt amount, as well as the time in which under the terms and conditions the debt should be paid. A promissory note is not necessarily linked with a deed of trust or a mortgage. It is basically a debt instrument. A debt instrument without any concrete collateral is known as an unsecured note. The lender or financial institution that holds the financial instrument is known as the payee and has the authority to transfer get payment to a third party when they sign the promissory note over to a third party.

Loan origination is the procedure involved of a mortgage application. A fee is charged for this service. It is also known as a loan origination fee. The government of the United States handles the fee as discount points against the costs associated with borrowing money. The discount points equate to 1% of the amount of the loan and are included in interest that is prepaid at the closing of the deal.

The deed of trust or mortgage document confirms the property's security for the debt (or mortgage) to a lender. These documents need to be signed by all parties and in writing in order to be legally binding.

In some circumstances the borrowers' may prefer to have a three-party instrument also known as a deed of trust, or a trust deed, instead of a mortgage. This document gives legal title to the property without ownership of the property. The third party is known as the trustee. They hold the rights to the title on behalf of the lender also known as the beneficiary. The promissory note is held by the beneficiary. If the trustor, or borrower, does not pay the debt this is a protection of the terms and the conditions written out in the deed.

There three basic types of foreclosure proceedings are strict foreclosure, judicial and nonjudicial. The terms and the conditions for each of these are different from each state to state within the United States. In terms of nonjudicial foreclosure, some states permit nonjudicial foreclosure processes to be used with the security instrument includes a power-of-sale clause. With this process, there is not any court action or legal action that is required.

With judicial foreclosure, the property is permitted to be sold through court order and after the mortgagee or borrower has provided sufficient public notification. When a mortgagee defaults, the lender can then accelerate the amount owing remaining principal of the debt, including any administrative costs, penalties and interest. The attorney for the lender can then file a lawsuit to foreclose the lien. There is a court proceeding and after a presentation of the facts and the circumstances, the property is then sentenced to be sold. There is a public sale where the property is held and advertised and the real estate is given to the buyer who is willing to purchase it at the highest price. Sole owner or joint tenant, or tenant by the entirety, sells or leases by statute, mortgage foreclosures can happen only through a court proceeding. In different states this is known as the Mortgage Foreclosure Law (735 ILCS 5/) and the term mortgage is inclusive.

There are moments when a borrower who has defaulted on their mortgage can have a chance for redemption in order to receive the equitable right of redemption. Before foreclosure, but after default, the borrower would pay the lender the amount in default, including the costs of the debt that will be reinstated for regular payments that begin again. Sometimes the person who redeems must repay the accelerated loan amount in full. In some states in the United States the defaulted borrower has a period of time to redeem their real estate after it has gone for sale, usually this time period could be one full calendar year in length. The borrower has a legal right of redemption.

Quiz

1. What is an acceleration clause?

2. What is an alienation clause?

3. What is a beneficiary?

4. What is a certificate of sale?

5. What is a deed in lieu of foreclosure?

6. What is a deed of trust?

7. What is a defeasance clause?

8. What is a deficiency judgment?

9. What is a discount point?

10. What is an equitable right of redemption?

11. What is an equitable title?

12. What is an escrow account?

13. What is foreclosure?

14. What is hypothecation?

15. What interest is as discussed in this chapter?

16. What is intermediate mortgage?

17. What is judicial foreclosure?

18. What is a land contract?

19. What is lien theory?

20. What is a loan origination fee?

21. What is a mortgage?

22. What is a mortgagee?

23. What is a mortgagor?

24. What is a negotiable instrument?

25. What is a non-judicial foreclosure?

26. What is novation?

27. What is prepayment penalty?

28. What is a promissory note?

29. What is a release deed?

30. What is satisfaction of mortgage?

31. What is a sheriff's deed?

32. What is a sheriff's sale?

33. What is a statutory right of redemption?

34. What is a statutory right of reinstatement?

35. What is a strict foreclosure?

36. What theory is as discussed in this chapter?

37. What is title theory?

38. What is usury?

CHAPTER NINE: COMMERCIAL REAL ESTATE

Commercial Real Estate Work

Commercial real estate can involve a lot of different kinds of work such as commercial retail (shops, stores, etc.), land (farmland and cattle land), malls (larger commercial real estate), combination residential and commercial real estate (someone lives above the space on the ground floor where the business is taking place. There are many different kinds of scenarios that would warrant a real estate professional to be involved with the work of commercial real estate, but the key thing is that all of commercial real estate involves real estate that is not for the purposes of living or for residing in – it is real estate with the purpose of doing business with the real estate.

License Requirements

Real estate professionals that want to also work in commercial real estate and residential real estate, or solely for commercial real estate or solely for residential real estate do not require a special license in order to do this. As discussed in previous chapters, particularly the first chapter, the license requirements for a real estate professional was discussed. A real estate professional who has met all of the requirements to obtain a real estate license can practice commercial real estate.

Types of Investment Property

Here are various types of investment property that landlords are hoping to earn the most income from:

- Unimproved land
- Residential
- Single-Family residences
- Small multi-family residences
- Large multi-family properties
- Office buildings
- Retail property
- Industrial and manufacturing properties

- Structural and site considerations
- Mixed-use buildings

Buying vs. Leasing

When a landowner decides to purchase the property, if they have that much collateral, this will maximize their profit on the property faster than leasing. For landowners who are making a long-term investment, purchasing or buying property is the best option.

If a potential purchaser is more interested in a shorter term investment in terms of the business they are running, for example it could be a yoga wear company and the owner is fully aware that yoga wear could be a fast buck, a passing phase, but not something that they could see realistically sustaining them for the rest of their life – then leasing a property would be the better option. As well, by leasing a property, as long as the sales that are derived, or the income earned from the business can cover the cost of the leasing expenses and still give the owner a profit, this is a desirable option as well. This would also help someone leasing commercial real estate to lease the property in a location that is very "hot" so-to-speak in the area where business tends to get a lot of foot traffic. Whereas a buyer of commercial property may need to purchase the business in a location that does not have as much foot traffic for their business, unless they have been in business for decades or even centuries. Commercial property that is bought is better done if it occurs more recently for businesses that do not depend on a lot of foot traffic from people passing by. For example, retail sales in fashion would be better done through leasing, whereas, a business that is concerning the manufacturing of toilets would be better purchased.

Owning Property

There are some key terms to know connected to owning property:
- Advantages for taxes
- Income
- Appreciation
- Property control

There are also disadvantages as well:
- Capital outlay initially

- Liability
- Financing
- Requirements for management
- Compliance legally
- Inflexibility

Amenity Purchase

An **amenity purchase** is an investor who wants to put in money where it will earn more money.

Leasing Property

The acquiring fee simple ownership is an alternative to obtaining a leasehold interest in property. Acquiring occupancy rights is leasing, physical and partial economic use of property for a specific period.

Some of the advantages of leasing include:
- Flexibility
- Lower up-front cash requirement
- Some tax relief (property taxes, rent, and other expenses are deductible)
- Lower risk of obsolescence
- Stability of costs
- Mobility
- Better return on inventory turnover as opposed to tying up capital in ownership
    Disadvantages include:
- Inability to take advantage of appreciation
- Inability to take advantage of tax deductible advantages, such as interest on mortgage loans and recognition of building depreciation
- Lack of control over property
- Lack of operational control and changes
- Limited tax relief

- Contractual penalties

Actual total cost of leasing is often more expensive per square foot than ownership.

Leaseback and Sale

This happens when a company holds the title to the property and can receive a profitable return on from their initial investment by providing the seller/occupants income in the company's freehold estate.

Long-term Lease on Land

A long-term lease on land can run from 10 to five years

Considerations for Lessors and Lessees

Here are some of the considerations to consider:
- Gross leases
- Net Leases
- Lease clauses
- Attornment
- Estoppel/Estoppel certificate
- Subordination and non-disturbance
- Utility clauses
- Insurance and property tax payments
- Lease structure
- Index leases
- Porter's wage escalation formula
- Disposal of leased space
- Good-guy clause
- Commercial commissions

- Sales

Leases

Here are the various forms of leases after a lump sum commission for the real estate professional:

- Per square foot fee
- Flat fee
- Procurement fee

Timing of Commercial Commissions

The payments may be periodic.

Summary

Commercial real estate can involve a lot of different kinds of work such as commercial retail (shops, stores, etc.), land (farmland and cattle land), malls (larger commercial real estate), combination residential and commercial real estate (someone lives above the space on the ground floor where the business is taking place. There are many different kinds of scenarios that would warrant a real estate professional to be involved with the work of commercial real estate, but the key thing is that all of commercial real estate involves real estate that is not for the purposes of living or for residing in – it is real estate with the purpose of doing business with the real estate.

Real estate professionals that want to also work in commercial real estate and residential real estate, or solely for commercial real estate or solely for residential real estate do not require a special license in order to do this. As discussed in previous chapters, particularly the first chapter, the license requirements for a real estate professional was discussed. A real estate professional who has met all of the requirements to obtain a real estate license can practice commercial real estate.

When a landowner decides to purchase the property, if they have that much collateral, this will maximize their profit on the property faster than leasing. For landowners who are making a long-term investment, purchasing or buying property is the best option.

If a potential purchaser is more interested in a shorter term investment in terms of the business they are running, for example it could be a yoga wear company and the owner is fully aware that yoga wear could be a fast buck, a passing phase, but not something that they could see realistically sustaining them for the rest of their life – then leasing a property would be the better option. As well, by leasing a property, as long as the sales that are derived, or the income earned from the business can cover the cost of the leasing expenses and still give the owner a profit, this is a desirable option as well. This would also help someone leasing commercial real estate to lease the property in a location that is very "hot" so-to-speak in the area where business tends to get a lot of foot traffic. Whereas a buyer of commercial property may need to purchase the business in a location that does not have as much foot traffic for their business, unless they have been in business for decades or even centuries. Commercial property that is bought is better done if it occurs more recently for businesses that do not depend on a lot of foot traffic from people passing by. For example, retail sales in fashion would be better done through leasing, whereas, a business that is concerning the manufacturing of toilets would be better purchased.

This happens when a company holds the title to the property and can receive a profitable return on from their initial investment by providing the seller/occupants income in the company's freehold estate.

Quiz

1. What is an amenity purchaser?

2. What is a buyer agency?

3. What is a Common Area Maintenance (CAM)?

4. What is a commercial broker's lien?

5. What is an escalation clause?

6. What is a graduated lease?

7. What is a gross lease?

8. What is a land lease?

9. What is a net lease?

10. What is a pass-through?

11. What is sale and leaseback?

12. What a setback is as discussed in this chapter?

13. What is a subdivision?

14. Why would someone consider purchasing commercial real estate?

15. What are the differences between buying a property and leasing a property?

CHAPTER 10: COMMERCIAL REAL ESTATE

Commercial Real Estate Work

Commercial real estate can involve a lot of different kinds of work such as commercial retail (shops, stores, etc.), land (farmland and cattle land), malls (larger commercial real estate), combination residential and commercial real estate (someone lives above the space on the ground floor where the business is taking place. There are many different kinds of scenarios that would warrant a real estate professional to be involved with the work of commercial real estate, but the key thing is that all of commercial real estate involves real estate that is not for the purposes of living or for residing in – it is real estate with the purpose of doing business with the real estate.

License Requirements

Real estate professionals that want to also work in commercial real estate and residential real estate, or solely for commercial real estate or solely for residential real estate do not require a special license in order to do this. As discussed in previous chapters, particularly the first chapter, the license requirements for a real estate professional was discussed. A real estate professional who has met all of the requirements to obtain a real estate license can practice commercial real estate.

Types of Investment Property

Here are various types of investment property that landlords are hoping to earn the most income from:
- Unimproved land
- Residential
- Single-Family residences
- Small multi-family residences
- Large multi-family properties
- Office buildings
- Retail property
- Industrial and manufacturing properties

- Structural and site considerations
- Mixed-use buildings

Buying vs. Leasing

When a landowner decides to purchase the property, if they have that much collateral, this will maximize their profit on the property faster than leasing. For landowners who are making a long-term investment, purchasing or buying property is the best option.

If a potential purchaser is more interested in a shorter term investment in terms of the business they are running, for example it could be a yoga wear company and the owner is fully aware that yoga wear could be a fast buck, a passing phase, but not something that they could see realistically sustaining them for the rest of their life – then leasing a property would be the better option. As well, by leasing a property, as long as the sales that are derived, or the income earned from the business can cover the cost of the leasing expenses and still give the owner a profit, this is a desirable option as well. This would also help someone leasing commercial real estate to lease the property in a location that is very "hot" so-to-speak in the area where business tends to get a lot of foot traffic. Whereas a buyer of commercial property may need to purchase the business in a location that does not have as much foot traffic for their business, unless they have been in business for decades or even centuries. Commercial property that is bought is better done if it occurs more recently for businesses that do not depend on a lot of foot traffic from people passing by. For example, retail sales in fashion would be better done through leasing, whereas, a business that is concerning the manufacturing of toilets would be better purchased.

Owning Property

There are some key terms to know connected to owning property:
- Advantages for taxes
- Income
- Appreciation
- Property control

There are also disadvantages as well:
- Capital outlay initially

- Liability
- Financing
- Requirements for management
- Compliance legally
- Inflexibility

Amenity Purchase

An **amenity purchase** is an investor who wants to put in money where it will earn more money.

Leasing Property

The acquiring fee simple ownership is an alternative to obtaining a leasehold interest in property. Acquiring occupancy rights is leasing, physical and partial economic use of property for a specific period.

Some of the advantages of leasing include:
- Flexibility
- Lower up-front cash requirement
- Some tax relief (property taxes, rent, and other expenses are deductible)
- Lower risk of obsolescence
- Stability of costs
- Mobility
- Better return on inventory turnover as opposed to tying up capital in ownership
    Disadvantages include:
- Inability to take advantage of appreciation
- Inability to take advantage of tax deductible advantages, such as interest on mortgage loans and recognition of building depreciation
- Lack of control over property
- Lack of operational control and changes
- Limited tax relief

- Contractual penalties

Actual total cost of leasing is often more expensive per square foot than ownership.

Leaseback and Sale

This happens when a company holds the title to the property and can receive a profitable return on from their initial investment by providing the seller/occupants income in the company's freehold estate.

Long-term Lease on Land

A long-term lease on land can run from 10 to five years

Considerations for Lessors and Lessees

Here are some of the considerations to consider:
- Gross leases
- Net Leases
- Lease clauses
- Attornment
- Estoppel/Estoppel certificate
- Subordination and non-disturbance
- Utility clauses
- Insurance and property tax payments
- Lease structure
- Index leases
- Porter's wage escalation formula
- Disposal of leased space
- Good-guy clause
- Commercial commissions

- Sales

Leases

Here are the various forms of leases after a lump sum commission for the real estate professional:
- Per square foot fee
- Flat fee
- Procurement fee

Timing of Commercial Commissions

The payments may be periodic.

Summary

Commercial real estate can involve a lot of different kinds of work such as commercial retail (shops, stores, etc.), land (farmland and cattle land), malls (larger commercial real estate), combination residential and commercial real estate (someone lives above the space on the ground floor where the business is taking place. There are many different kinds of scenarios that would warrant a real estate professional to be involved with the work of commercial real estate, but the key thing is that all of commercial real estate involves real estate that is not for the purposes of living or for residing in – it is real estate with the purpose of doing business with the real estate.

Real estate professionals that want to also work in commercial real estate and residential real estate, or solely for commercial real estate or solely for residential real estate do not require a special license in order to do this. As discussed in previous chapters, particularly the first chapter, the license requirements for a real estate professional was discussed. A real estate professional who has met all of the requirements to obtain a real estate license can practice commercial real estate.

When a landowner decides to purchase the property, if they have that much collateral, this will maximize their profit on the property faster than leasing. For landowners who are making a long-term investment, purchasing or buying property is the best option.

If a potential purchaser is more interested in a shorter term investment in terms of the business they are running, for example it could be a yoga wear company and the owner is fully aware that yoga wear could be a fast buck, a passing phase, but not something that they could see realistically sustaining them for the rest of their life – then leasing a property would be the better option. As well, by leasing a property, as long as the sales that are derived, or the income earned from the business can cover the cost of the leasing expenses and still give the owner a profit, this is a desirable option as well. This would also help someone leasing commercial real estate to lease the property in a location that is very "hot" so-to-speak in the area where business tends to get a lot of foot traffic. Whereas a buyer of commercial property may need to purchase the business in a location that does not have as much foot traffic for their business, unless they have been in business for decades or even centuries. Commercial property that is bought is better done if it occurs more recently for businesses that do not depend on a lot of foot traffic from people passing by. For example, retail sales in fashion would be better done through leasing, whereas, a business that is concerning the manufacturing of toilets would be better purchased.

This happens when a company holds the title to the property and can receive a profitable return on from their initial investment by providing the seller/occupants income in the company's freehold estate.

Quiz

16. What is an amenity purchaser?

17. What is a buyer agency?

18. What is a Common Area Maintenance (CAM)?

19. What is a commercial broker's lien?

20. What is an escalation clause?

21. What is a graduated lease?

22. What is a gross lease?

23. What is a land lease?

24. What is a net lease?

25. What is a pass-through?

26. What is sale and leaseback?

27. What a setback is as discussed in this chapter?

28. What is a subdivision?

29. Why would someone consider purchasing commercial real estate?

30. What are the differences between buying a property and leasing a property?

www.ingramcontent.com/pod-product-compliance
Lightning Source LLC
Chambersburg PA
CBHW022015170526
45157CB00003B/1255